SO-DFZ-029

THE GREAT LIVES SERIES

Great Lives biographies shed an exciting new light on the many dynamic men and women whose actions, visions, and dedication to an ideal have influenced the course of history. Their ambitions, dreams, successes and failures, the controversies they faced and the obstacles they overcame are the true stories behind these distinguished world leaders, explorers, and great Americans.

Other biographies in the Great Lives Series

CLARA BARTON: *Founder of the*
American Red Cross
CHRISTOHPER COLUMBUS: *The Intrepid Mariner*
AMELIA EARHART: *Challenging the Skies*
THOMAS EDISON: *Inventing the Future*
JOHN GLENN: *Space Pioneer*
MIKHAIL GORBACHEV: *The Soviet Innovator*
JESSE JACKSON: *A Voice for Change*
JOHN F. KENNEDY: *Courage in Crisis*
MARTIN LUTHER KING: *Dreams for a Nation*
ABRAHAM LINCOLN: *The Freedom President*
NELSON MANDELA: *A Voice Set Free*
GOLDA MEIR: *A Leader in Peace and War*
SALLY RIDE: *Shooting for the Stars*
FRANKLIN D. ROOSEVELT: *The People's President*
HARRIET TUBMAN: *Call to Freedom*

A special thanks to educators Dr. Frank Moretti, Ph.D., Associate Headmaster of the Dalton School in New York City; Dr. Paul Mattingly, Ph.D., Professor of History at New York University; and Barbara Smith, M.S., Assistant Superintendent of the Los Angeles Unified School District, for their contributions to the Great Lives Series.

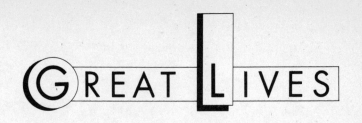

SANDRA DAY O'CONNOR
A New Justice, a New Voice

Beverly Berwald

FAWCETT COLUMBINE
NEW YORK

TABLE OF CONTENTS

Chapter 1
 Facing the Senate · 1

Chapter 2
 Girl on the Ranch · 11

Chapter 3
 Defying the Odds · 27

Chapter 4
 Job Hunt and Marriage · 35

Chapter 5
 Starting a Family · 41

Chapter 6
 The Peaceful Activist · 51

Chapter 7
 Old-fashioned Justice · 63

Chapter 8
 A Woman for All Seasons · 75

Chapter 9
 Last Stop, The Supreme Court · 87

Chapter 10
 A Voice for the Future · 101

Appendix · 115
Bibliography · 121

1

Facing the Senate

ON THE NINTH of September, 1981, a sea of reporters and cameramen rushed toward a small, trim 51-year-old woman as she climbed the steps to the nation's Capitol. Her name was Sandra Day O'Connor, and her fate was in the hands of eighteen senators who waited inside the building to question her. Their job was to advise their colleagues in the Senate on the president's nominee for the first woman justice of the U. S. Supreme Court.

The anticipation was nerve-wracking. Though her heart was pounding, Sandra Day O'Connor was an island of calm. A tough pioneering spirit blazed behind her hazel eyes, showing the determination and pluck that saw her rope a steer when she was nine, graduate from college in three years, raise three sons, start a law practice, work as assistant attorney general, a state senator, a judge on the Arizona Superior Court, and then the Court of Appeals.

Members of the media continued to jostle for a position as she stepped through the north entrance to the Rotunda. O'Connor passed the mosaics and paintings depicting scenes from the Revolutionary War. Her path to the Senate committee room was the same one that had been walked by other distinguished Supreme Court nominees, such as Roger Taney (1836–1864), the first Catholic justice, Louis Brandeis (1916–1939), the first Jewish Supreme Court Judge, and, more currently, Thurgood Marshall (1967), the first black to serve on the high court.

A sense of relief came over O'Connor when she spotted Senator Barry Goldwater striding down the hallway with Senator Strom Thurmond, the chairman of the Senate Judiciary Committee. Goldwater, one of O'Connor's best friends, took great pride in her accomplishments. He had never known a person more brilliant or more scrupulously fair. He took her left arm while Senator Thurmond took her right, and they escorted her to the committee hearings.

All the senators and congressmen work together to make the laws governing the citizens of the United States. But the senators also have the task of confirming or denying the president's choices for the U. S. Supreme Court, the most powerful court in the land that interprets our constitutional rights.

Since 1789, 101 justices have served on the U. S. Supreme Court. All had been men. President Ronald Reagan had promised during his 1980 election campaign to appoint a woman to the U. S. Supreme Court. He followed through on his pledge by nominating Sandra Day

O'Connor to the Court. It was hailed across the country as a major breakthrough for women, who have struggled many years to attain full equality in American society. However, the President's nomination was not final. It had to be confirmed by the Senate.

Inside the committee room O'Connor took her seat before the senators. Spectators packed the room, bringing with them an air of excitement and celebration. A faint smile crossed her face as she thought about the number of times she had sat in judgement over a defendant in court. Now it was her turn to be judged, not by one person, but by eighteen senators. Their gray suits contrasted somberly with the mahogany desks and the red carpet decorated with gold stars. Under the blinding spotlights, O'Connor thought back to the moment two months earlier, when her life had taken an abrupt change.

She was one of nine judges on the Arizona State Court of Appeals and she had been sitting in her chambers writing an opinion. The weather was unseasonably hot, even for Arizona in July. The phone rang, shattering her concentration. It was President Reagan calling to find out if O'Connor, a conservative like himself, would accept the nomination for associate justice of the Supreme Court. Justice Potter Stewart was retiring after twenty-three years of service on the high court, and she would be his replacement.

Almost as soon as she said yes, she had been besieged by reporters, photographers, and cameramen. Secret Service men even came from Washington to protect her and her family as she prepared for the Senate hearings. She had to be ready to field questions on every case she'd ever ruled on. It was worse than cramming for a final exam. Her husband, friends, and four assistant law clerks drilled her relentlessly on thirty years of legal cases. On top of it, she had to review volumes of recent Supreme Court decisions and the written records of other confirmation hearings. As usual O'Connor had tackled the job with boundless energy, quietly but steadily preparing herself for what lay ahead.

In the Senate committee room, Senator Thurmond slammed the gavel down, wrenching O'Connor back to the present. A hush descended over the room. The television cameras began to whir as Senator Thurmond introduced O'Connor. She braced herself for a surge of adrenaline. Her voice was calm and clear, and she began to speak about the marriage ceremony she had so often performed as judge. It was her way of honoring the family she'd grown up in, and her own family of her husband and three sons. Their love and support were no small part of her accomplishments. Believing that the family is the smallest unit of society, O'Connor stressed its importance for the future of the world.

Then Sandra Day O'Connor introduced each member of her family, beaming with pride. She talked briefly about their accomplishments. Scott, the oldest, was a graduate of Stanford, a state swimming champion, a pilot, and a young businessman. Brian, her second son, was a senior at Colorado College and an adventur-

4

er/skydiver with 400 jumps. Her youngest son, Jay, was a sophomore at Stanford, and an excellent skier and golfer. As a capable writer, he had become her assistant press secretary after her nomination. Finally, she introduced her husband of twenty-nine years, John O'Connor, as an infinite source of enthusiasm.

Slowly the senators began to bombard her with questions on controversial issues such as school busing, crime, the death penalty, and abortion. School busing had been used as a way of remedying racial discrimination in many states. However, O'Connor hesitated to endorse this as a practical solution because of her concern for children. When she was in junior high school, she took a bus seventy-five miles round-trip from her parents' remote ranch to school every day. The memory was all too vivid and disturbing.

When asked about the high crime rate in our country, O'Connor spoke about the general breakdown in the standards of morality. Not content with a quick summary of such a serious problem, she delved deeply into some of the reasons for it. Families were splitting up as quickly as they came together. A changing, nomadic society prevented Americans from ever knowing their neighbors too well. A lack of bonding among people deprived the individual of peer guidance to help shape ideas of what is right or wrong. Easy access to drugs also fanned the problem of crime.

Once the reasons for crime were clarified, O'Connor addressed the need for more prisons to separate the unlawful from the innocent in society. She feared that lim-

5

ited prison space would force the states to release criminals with five-year sentences within a three-month
period. In admitting there were no easy answers to the
problem, O'Connor suggested that the lawmakers might
explore some solutions among themselves.

When she answered her gentlemen inquisitors on the
death penalty, she was swift and certain. As a state
senator she had worked extensively on writing a fair
law that would bring back the death penalty, after the
Supreme Court had overturned the old laws as cruel
and unusual punishment in 1972.

The most fiery issue, however, was abortion. The U.
S. Supreme Court decision of 1973, Roe v. Wade, had
given women the legal right to abortion without inter-
ference from the government. The anti-abortion movement was seeking to overthrow that decision. Those in
favor of a woman's right to chose, the pro-choice advocates, believe that personal religious or philosophical
beliefs—not the government—should dictate an individual's decision on abortion. They also believe an unwanted pregnancy can be a terrible hardship on single
or underaged women who cannot afford to raise a child.
Senator Jeremiah Denton of Alabama badgered
O'Connor on the subject. He wanted a firm commitment
for or against abortion.

If O'Connor's answers to abortion questions erupted
into a heated controversy, her chances for the Supreme
Court would be lost. She summoned all her wisdom to
balance on this difficult tightrope. Folding her hands

tightly and reigning in her nervousness, she paused before answering.

"I'm opposed to abortion as birth control or other-
wise," Connor finally began. "However," she pointed
out, "I'm not going to be pregnant anymore, so it's easy
for me to hold that position."

She was clear to separate her own opinions from the
rights of others. Then she apologized to the committee
members, but insisted she could not reveal how she
would vote on abortion. It would be unethical, she said,
to prejudice an issue by taking a stand on it before it
came up in court. She was quick to draw on ethical tradition by reminding the Senators that other past nominees to the Supreme Court had similarly declined comment on issues that might come before the Court.

At the end of her testimony O'Connor felt satisfied.
She had not allowed herself to be backed into a corner.
She was fairly certain that no one could possibly use
anything she had said against her. She breathed a sigh
of relief at how smoothly things seemed to be going.

The American Bar Association (ABA) representatives praised her for her professional competence. Although they concluded there were other women in the
law who had more experience than O'Connor, they ap-
plauded her diverse background. The ABA gave her
their seal of approval.

Though the National Organization for Women
(NOW), which had been fighting for women's rights
since 1966, did not agree with all of O'Connor's legal
and political views, they also supported her nomina-

tion. Eleanor Smeal, who was president of NOW, spoke encouragingly about her. The organization was pleased with O'Connor's work, as a lawmaker and a judge, in helping to abolish discrimination against women and minorities.

When the anti-abortion contingency showed up in the committee room, however, a wave of anxiety swept over O'Connor. The pro-life advocates tried to muster support from Jesse Helms, the North Carolina Republican and religious conservative, but President Reagan had already assured Senator Helms that O'Connor was not a staunch supporter of the ERA or abortion. However, the anti-abortionists could not forget what O'Connor had done in 1974. As Arizona state senator, seven years earlier, she had voted against a bill urging Congress to pass a Human Life Amendment. The amendment would have made abortion illegal throughout the United States, except when a woman's life was endangered. O'Connor had also voted to continue funding abortions with state taxes at the University of Arizona Hospital. Despite her opposition, the funds were cut off. O'Connor's pro-abortion stand in this matter was still a sore spot with anti-abortionists. O'Connor took a deep breath as the room began to stir while the anti-abortionists spoke. The senators grew restless. Some were bored. One by one they quietly stood up and walked out on the anti-abortionists! They had been O'Connor's only real opposition, and their strength had evaporated before her eyes.

After three days the hearings adjourned. Though

8

UPI/Bettmann Newsphotos

One of President Reagan's campaign promises in the 1980 presidential election had been to appoint a woman to the Supreme Court, and with Sandra Day O'Connor's nomination he kept that promise. In July 1981, O'Connor visited with the president in the rose garden at the White House. Each confessed that their happiest moments were spent on western ranches, riding horses and roping steers.

9

O'Connor felt encouraged, she did not know whether she had made it to the bench. She went back to Arizona with her family, gripped by uncertainty.

A few days later the full Senate confirmed President Reagan's nominee to the Supreme Court. It had been a long and winding journey for Sandra that had begun on a remote ranch in Duncan, Arizona. She had defied existing barriers by having ambitions that were considered unacceptable for women. She lived by a simple axiom, that knowledge and hard work could elevate a person above the issue of being male or female. In the best American tradition, Sandra Day O'Connor is a pioneer.

2

Girl on the Ranch

MOUNTAINS, DESERTS, AND broad river valleys come together in a common thirst for water; scarce in the hot, dry land called Arizona. Men who survived the furnace-like heat were forged of iron strength. They were living examples of a philosophy known as rugged individualism, a belief in the strength of each person to pull oneself through any crisis. These same pioneers endured great hardship to build new lives. The ancestors of Sandra Day O'Connor were just such pioneers.

Over a hundred years ago, in the 1880s, Sandra's grandfather Henry Clay (H.C.) Day left the lush, green hills of Vermont and traveled west. He was only twenty-one when he first settled in Wichita, Kansas, but he was enterprising. After turning a few solid deals in lumber and real estate, he had earned a small fortune. His confidence soared. He could afford to marry his sweetheart, Alice Edith Hilton, and start a family. Since Alice's parents had died many years earlier, she had been raised by friends of the family, the Fishers. Judge Fisher regaled Henry with true stories about the territory of Arizona. There was plenty of water from the rushing Gila River. The grass was tall and thick, just right for grazing cattle. Since it was public domain, anyone could use the land. Judge Fisher encouraged Henry to invest his money in cattle.

Sandra Day O'Connor's grandfather leaped at the opportunity and formed a partnership with the Fishers' son, Lane. Henry put up the money and Lane took care of purchasing 6,000 head of cattle, which he drove across the Mexican border into Arizona. The cattle were free to roam on 155,000 acres, staked out by Henry Day as the Lazy B ranch. The nearest town was Duncan, and that was twenty miles away.

The Southern Pacific Railroad was completed through Lordsburg, New Mexico, in 1882, just in time for Henry to bring his young wife, Alice, out from Kansas. It was another twenty-five miles on horseback from Lordsburg to the ranch. When Alice arrived at their adobe home she was surprised at how close it was to the Gila River. She also soon learned that Apaches, led by the famous warrior Geronimo, were attacking ranchers. The Apaches resented the white settlers for invading their land. They sought revenge by stealing horses. The Days lost many that way, but fortunately they survived the attacks unscathed.

When Geronimo surrendered in 1886, they breathed a sigh of relief, but for only a short while. The Lazy B was soon hit by a series of flash floods. One torrential downpour washed out their adobe house, carrying their grand piano away. The flood left H.C. and Alice homeless with four small children to look after. The Days briefly considered selling the ranch, but instead they toughened their resolve to stick it out. It was a trait they would pass on to future generations. H.C. and Alice moved their family to higher ground and built their second home. In 1898 Alice gave birth to their fifth child, Harry, who would eventually become Sandra's father.

The Lazy B was so remote that H.C. was afraid his children would grow up without an education, so he built a one-room schoolhouse and hired a live-in teacher. Eventually the Days left the ranch and moved to Pasadena, California, where Harry finished high school. Bursting with ambition, young Harry decided to attend a brand new university called Stanford. Fate intervened, however, when Harry got word that the Lazy B was going under.

H.C. had died and his partners had run out of money. Harry gave up his plans to attend Stanford and went to Arizona to rescue the ranch. Everywhere he turned at the sprawling Lazy B, he saw ruination. Fences need to be repaired, windmills reconstructed, corrals rebuilt. His sister Eleanor urged him to give it up, but, like his father, Harry was not a quitter. He was challenged by the prospect of turning ill fortune into good luck.

For the next ten years, he labored eighteen-hour days to get the Lazy B back on its feet. Prosperity slowly returned to the ranch. When he married Ada Mae Wilkey, he married a source of encouragement. Ada Mae was as strong as she was elegant and sophisticated. She had spent many years in the city of El Paso, Texas, remarkably cosmopolitan for the 1920s. At sixteen, she had traveled throughout Europe on a tour with an English class. By the time she graduated from the University of Arizona, she was known for her beautiful soprano voice and her ability on the piano. The harsh life on the ranch was a far cry from the comforts of El Paso, but Ada Mae was so in love with Harry that her decision was easy. She moved into the four-room adobe house with no running water, no electricity, no indoor plumbing—and never regretted it.

Three years into their marriage, Ada Mae became pregnant with her first child. Since there were no doctors near the ranch, she moved back to El Paso to live with her mother, Mamie. On March 26, 1930, the same day that Harry was in a Tucson court settling the property matter, Ada Mae was in an El Paso hospital giving birth to Sandra. A month later, Ada Mae was ready to bring the baby home to the Lazy B. Harry was concerned that his wife and new daughter would be exposed to a life of hardship on the ranch, but Ada Mae insisted the family be together. She missed her husband, and she knew that all the cowhands depended upon her, too. She returned to the ranch with baby Sandra and to a full-time job of mothering, cooking, and cleaning.

Ada Mae never complained about all the years of hauling water before Harry installed plumbing in their house in 1937. Her enduring nature was a study of grace

14

under pressure. She had a quiet though powerful influence upon her young daughter. Sandra later displayed the same calm strength when she was thrust into the public eye with her nomination to the Supreme Court.

Despite her chores, Ada Mae Day always managed to carve out time to read. Her hunger for intellectual stimulation had her subscribing to books, magazines, and the newspapers from the major American cities. One of Sandra's earliest memories was of her mother reading to her from the *Book of Knowledge* and *National Geographic.* Young Sandra developed a vivid imagination as she listened to stories about people halfway around the globe in Europe, Asia, and Africa. She developed a respect for differences among individuals. This evolved into her belief that people should be free to govern themselves locally. It was a conviction that would command her loyalty through the years.

Soon young Sandra was reading on her own, having mastered the Calvert method, a home study course taught by her mother. Then a spate of bad luck hit the Lazy B ranch in the 1930s. Droughts left the ranch with dying crops and sickly cattle. Harry was so scared he stashed away five hundred dollars just in case they had to abandon the ranch. The Days' only hope was a man from Imperial Valley, California, who offered to buy up their cows for a cent and a half per pound. Harry and Ada Mae were grateful for the offer. However, when the buyer arrived, he took one look at Harry's emaciated livestock and canceled the deal. It was a devastating blow to the Days. It looked as though they'd have to give up.

Fortunately, it was the decade of the New Deal, an array of economic, employment, and social welfare programs that President Roosevelt initiated to lead America out of the Great Depression. The New Deal rescued the Days, along with many other farmers across America. Though Harry believed in individualism, he knew Roosevelt's program was his last hope. The federal government paid Harry twelve dollars a head for his ailing cows and twenty for the healthy ones worth shipping. As a result, the Lazy B was pulled back from the brink of ruin.

To help matters, Harry sent away for information on solar energy as a good, cheap source of energy. The University of California had been experimenting with harnessing the sun's power. Harry applied their research and his mechanical expertise to building solar heaters for the Lazy B. True to their pioneer spirit, the Days were some of the first people in this country to use this source of energy.

The Lazy B ranch, with its wide open land, gave Sandra a broad perspective on life. She developed a belief that there were few barriers in life, a belief which became a source of strength. It would serve her well in years to come when law firms refused to hire her because she was a woman. Sandra was also learning a lot about self-sufficiency on the ranch. When something broke down, her family couldn't call someone to fix it. The nearest road was eight miles away, and then it was another twenty miles to the closest town. Since the Day family didn't have the luxury of turning to hired strangers for help, they relied upon each other, including the cowhands who lived on the ranch. If a fence needed mending or a gate repaired, the whole family pitched in to help.

Ranch life was no respecter of gender. Sandra was expected to work on the Lazy B like all the other cowhands. She followed her father around, learning to ride a horse, rope a steer, or tend to sick cattle. Since there weren't any children within miles of the ranch, Sandra's friends were pet cats, horses, goats, and raccoons. Having developed a comfortable rapport with the cowboys, Sandra felt very much at ease when later she entered the field of law, a profession dominated by men. A sense of community developed out of necessity at the Lazy B. It was that spirit of participation that led Sandra to volunteer for public service when she left the ranch and started her own family.

One of the major drawbacks to living on an isolated ranch is the absence of schools. Ada Mae and Harry were concerned that their daughter have a good education. When Sandra was five years old, they drove her to El Paso to live with Grandmother Mamie Wilkey. When Ada and Harry climbed into the car for their trip back to Arizona, Sandra watched her folks drive away with sadness in her eyes. She probably would have loved nothing more than to spend the rest of her life on the ranch, but her mother and father believed that an education would give their daughter many more options in life.

El Paso was vastly different from the Lazy B ranch. It was a bustling city full of cattle traders like Sandra's Grandfather Wilkey. Solid brick homes lined Tularosa Avenue, the street where Sandra lived with her grandparents. When Grandmother Mamie Wilkey went into the kitchen she always came up with the most delicious concoctions. Though she was always homesick for her mother and father, Sandra felt loved and supported in this warm atmosphere. She thought of Grandmother Wilkey as a second mother. She looked up to her because her ideas of right and wrong were so firmly held. Grandmother Wilkey never hesitated to speak up when she disagreed with anyone.

Young Sandra found it exhilarating to be around this older woman, whose spirit was energetic and fearless. Her grandmother's independence was legendary. As a young girl of thirteen, she rode at the head of a wagon train that included her own family. Her father had decided to relocate to Sonora his freight service to the mines of Chihuahua, Mexico. In going from east to west, they had to traverse the Sierra Madre. With horses, wagons, and cattle, they negotiated this high, rugged range. Mamie was the first in the group to get to the top of the Sierra Madre and spot the other side.

Ambitious and hardworking, young Mamie was a pillar of strength to her family and the rest of the wagon party. They all relied on her Spanish to help them communicate along the way. Later on, when Grandmother

18

Mamie Wilkey's husband died, he left her three ranches. During the worst of the Depression, she couldn't afford to pay the bank notes on two of them. Sandra's father advised her to hold onto them. The banks were aware that most folks couldn't pay the mortgages. But Grandmother Wilkey didn't like to owe anybody money. She ran her own life and she wanted to keep it that way. She marched right into the bank and told the bankers to keep the deeds on two of the ranches. Her forceful personality left quite an impression on young Sandra. She would draw on her grandmother's example when she entered government later in life.

Each morning, Grandmother Wilkey drove Sandra five miles across town to the Radford School. It was a private girls school located in a quiet section of El Paso. Kindergarten turned out to be more fun than Sandra anticipated. She became friends with her cousin, Flournoy Davis, who was the daughter of Ada Mae's sister, Eleanor. They shared so much together they were like sisters. The only difference between the two of them were their looks, with Flournoy's blond braids in sharp contrast to Sandra's short, dark hair. When Sandra switched to public school for first and second grade, Flournoy did too. From then on, the girls were inseparable. In third grade, Sandra and Flournoy returned to the Radford School, where the classes of eight to ten students were more intimate.

The teachers at Radford were enthusiastic about teaching, and Sandra was eager to learn. She ploughed

19

through her homework the same way she had once tackled her chores on the ranch—thoroughly. She was so prepared when she went to class she absorbed the daily lessons faster than anyone else. Her teachers saw that she was moving at a rapid pace and advanced her one grade. The humble youngster thought nothing of it. She'd already learned on the ranch that you did the best you could without expecting any loud applause. A quiet self-confidence gained from a task well done was the best reward of all.

One teacher in particular, Miss Fireoved, who taught drama, inspired Sandra with her lively instruction in theater. She told her students that regardless of the role they would be playing, they must always be themselves. It was exciting for young Sandra to act on stage. She learned to project her voice and develop stage presence. Miss Fireoved's other class was a variation on drama, the art of impromptu speaking. Before lunch, all the students were given topics. They had less than an hour to prepare. When they returned from lunch they had to speak before the class as though they were experts. It was quite frightening for most of the girls, but Sandra found it thrilling. She seemed to have a knack for organizing what she wanted to say and then saying it calmly. It helped her to think and speak quickly and succinctly. This training was invaluable when she became an attorney and, later, a judge.

As much as Sandra loved the challenges at school, she lived for summers on the Lazy B. Sandra always boarded the train home with her cousin Flournoy. She looked forward to sitting around the dining room table with her family. Her father and mother were curious about the world outside and they expressed their opinions daily. This give-and-take communication helped young Sandra to express her own ideas about life outside the ranch.

Sandra was lucky to have Fluornoy's companionship during the summer. The two girls rode all over the ranch and as far as Cottonwood Canyon, where they discovered Indian pictographs on the stone embankments. They felt like young explorers, trying to decipher tribal language from an ancient civilization. Once they strayed far from the center of the ranch and got lost, but Sandra never panicked. She knew getting flustered would accomplish nothing. She quickly found a solution by following the pasture fences all the way back to the Lazy B.

Her days were long and wonderful as she swam and fished with Flournoy in the large water tanks on the ranch. When they tired of the outdoors, they'd go inside the house to the Days' extensive library. The girls would read to each other from Los Angeles newspapers like the *Los Angeles Times* or the *Wall Street Journal,* and from magazines like the *Saturday Evening Post.* Sandra and Fluornoy became more and more attached to the Lazy B.

One year, the two girls couldn't bear the thought of going back to El Paso. They thought that if they hid in the stock tank where they swam no one would find them. But Sandra's father heard them splashing around

21

as he called out to them. They answered him with a round of giggles. Harry told them to come down, but when they refused he roped them out with a lariat.

Once back at Radford, Sandra continued to earn excellent grades in her classes. English was one of her favorite subjects. Sandra routinely devoured books of all kinds, novels as well as biographies. One story in particular caught young Sandra's eye: the life of Clare Boothe Luce, the wife of the editor of *Life* magazine, Henry Luce. Sandra was fascinated by this woman's achievements. Clare Booth Luce had been a journalist, a playwright on Broadway, a U. S. congresswoman, and an ambassador. In her calm, self-assured way, she had pushed back the frontiers for women in politics and diplomacy. Every time young Sandra read of Clare Booth Luce's newest accomplishment, she became emboldened once again with the belief that there were no obstacles in life.

She was also inquisitive about history. She loved to read about the way civilizations developed throughout the world. Her horizons were further broadened when she joined the Melody Club in fifth grade. Her appreciation for music would serve her the rest of her life, as a relaxing retreat from all her personal and professional demands.

By the time Sandra was eight, her sister Ann was born. Two years later, her brother Alan arrived to offer companionship for Ann. While Sandra only saw them during summer vacations, she quickly established herself as a third parent. When they went on family vacations together, Sandra watched out for her younger siblings. She sized up a situation quickly and steered them away from possible danger. The Days were an adventurous family. They climbed mountains that were 10,000 feet high or picnicked along the Gila River. One summer they took a banana boat cruise throughout the Caribbean, where they stopped and toured exotic ports. Another summer the family was readying themselves for a cruise to Alaska. They'd already purchased their steamship tickets, but at the last minute the steamship workers went on strike. The Day family quickly solved the problem by renting a smaller boat and hiring a crew. Then they carried on with their original plans and cruised the inland passages.

Again Sandra learned to identify with solutions, not problems. She would use the same approach later on when, as a state senator, she steered her fellow lawmakers toward resolving their difficulties. Young Sandra's vacations with her family taught her something else of equal importance: It is important to strike a balance between work and play; life can be enjoyed without being deflected from one's goals.

As Sandra was preparing to enter eighth grade, she decided to try living on the ranch and going to a local school. It was a test of her endurance. She arose each morning while it was still dark. Her mother and father drove her to a highway eight miles away to catch a bus. It was another twenty-five miles to school, in Lordsburg, New Mexico. By winter, with the days growing shorter, Sandra would arrive home well after dark.

Each morning she awoke exhausted from the previous day's travels. She found very little time in which to do her homework. Though it was her choice from the start, she felt it was a poor use of time and energy. She never forgot this experience, and later it influenced her opinion against school busing as a way of achieving racial equality.

When she returned to the Radford School in El Paso a year later, all her friends were amazed at the transformation. A pudgy, little girl had grown into a tall and elegant teenager, faintly reminiscent of a gazelle. Even though she was reserved and shy, it didn't stem her interest in boys. She decided to transfer to coed Austin High. It was a big switch from an all-girls school.

Sandra's parents continued to extend their hospitality to her friends. It was not uncommon for Sandra to bring back three or four girlfriends from high school to spend the summer on the Lazy B. They were always treated to spectacular displays of lightning streaking across the sky and thunderstorms in the middle of the desert. They'd rise early in the morning to saddle up the horses and roam the ranch with Sandra's father, repairing fences and fixing windmills.

Though the city girls were excited by the chance to be cowgirls, they were even more thrilled when Sandra showed them a more stylish side of ranch life. Sandra and her friends amused themselves by dressing up in some of the latest fashions from Ada Mae's closet. Supper at the end of the day was always spiced with lively conversation. Sandra often helped out with the cooking.

24

Having absorbed some of the secrets from two great cooks, her mother and her grandmother, she was developing into a very fine cook herself. She often displayed her skills at large family gatherings. Preparing several dishes at once never bothered Sandra, since it was a good test of her efficiency.

By the time she was sixteen, Sandra had completed all the requirements for her high school diploma. Her heart was set on going to Stanford University, the same school her father had hoped to attend. However, Austin High School overlooked giving her a college entrance exam. Despite Sandra's accelerated pace and her honor grades, it never occurred to the high school administration that Sandra was destined for higher learning. None of the other students had shown any interest in going to college.

Other obstacles lay on Sandra's path to Stanford. The competition was keen. Only a fraction of the number of students in most colleges and universities were women then. The year was 1949 and thousands of World War II soldiers were coming home, ready to resume their lives where they left off. These men were given first preference by the universities. Having seen hard times and weathered them, the Day family was enjoying a little prosperity of its own, but their bankbook was no match for the wealthy families of most Stanford students.

Somehow the odds never chipped away at Sandra's determination. She had come from a family of hardy pioneers. It seemed only natural that she would continue the tradition. She was determined to push back the barriers against higher education for women. She applied to Stanford, and her belief that she would be admitted never wavered. Her enthusiasm and self-confidence were grounded in the knowledge that she had thoroughly prepared herself every step along the way.

Sandra triumphed over the odds and was admitted to Stanford University. Her academic record was outstanding and her list of extracurricular activities long. The university had no idea that their decision to admit this woman would have so many far-reaching consequences in the years to come.

3

Defying the Odds

WHEN SANDRA ENTERED Stanford University, she stepped into a world that was very different from El Paso. It was electrifying to be surrounded by other young people with challenging minds.

While most of the other female students had already decided upon a profession in education, Sandra had not yet decided which career she would choose. She thought English might be a possible major. Her mother had taught her to love books ever since she was a toddler, but Sandra was exploring other horizons, too. She studied geology, the science of the earth's crust.

She also considered following in her father's footsteps as a rancher. In order to run a ranch as a business, you had to know more than just how to rope a steer or lasso a horse. Ranching was a full-time job. Eventually, Sandra decided to study economics to learn how to develop her business skills. A woman in economics was unusual in the early 1950s. After all, in many states a husband still had the power to manage the family finances without the approval of his wife. Major corporations were run by men, except for rare women such as Helena Rubinstein, who ruled a cosmetics empire. On the whole, woman were not expected to know about financial matters, and they were certainly discouraged from learning about economics.

Sandra focused all her energy on her chosen major, spending long hours pouring over pages of things like cost accounting. She always made sure she was well prepared, so she could be confident when she spoke out in class. Astonished by her knowledge, Sandra's professors looked forward to hearing her comments. She had a much more complete grasp of the subject than most of the other students. Quickly she earned a reputation for doing the best job she could, and her grades reflected that.

University life was not just spent in the pursuit of knowledge. Sandra rewarded herself for her hard work by going out in the evenings with friends. Her favorite pastimes were movies, dancing, and dinner away from the dormitory. Sometimes on weekends she went skiing in Yosemite with friends, an exhilarating break after being in class all week long. With her ready smile and her refreshing sense of humor, Sandra was often invited to friends' homes during semester break. When she returned the invitations, her girlfriends leaped at the chance to visit the Lazy B. The Day ranch seemed like the Wild West to city folk.

Sandra timed her visits to coincide with roundup,

which happened twice a year when they harvested the cattle. The air bristled with excitement and neighboring ranchers came to help out. Before the sun even peaked over the horizon, Sandra and her girlfriends had to saddle up their horses alongside the cowboys and ride out to the rangeland where the cattle had been roaming all year long. They were among the riders who gathered the milling and bawling cattle, and drove them to the sorting area. There the cattle were separated into three categories. Some were destined for the marketplace, others were sold for breeding purposes, and the remaining went back to grazing a while longer. Roundup was a test of everyone's endurance. The days were long and exhausting, and Sandra's father was surprised to find out that Sandra's girlfriends from the city were up to the challenge.

An important event in Sandra's undergraduate life at college occurred when she enrolled in a course in business law, taught by Professor Harry Rathbun. Her years on the Lazy B and with her Grandmother Wilkey had given her the ability to come up with swift solutions that were always fair toward everyone involved. Studying with Professor Rathbun, she became fascinated in how people decided whether or not something was honest and just.

Professor Rathbun's teachings made Sandra interested in studying law. Stanford University had just begun a program that allowed students to finish their fourth year of college at the same time that they started their first year of law school. Since Sandra thrived on

29

challenges, the program appealed to her. Excited by her ambition, her father and mother encouraged her to enroll. But a friend of Sandra's father said she'd never be admitted. He reminded the Days that only a very small number of law students were women. Before the turn of the century, women weren't even allowed to practice law in many states.

Sandra was not discouraged, and her family kept up their hopes for her. Her grades were excellent and the Stanford faculty gave her a glowing recommendation. Because of this, Sandra was able to overcome the barriers against women, and the following fall Sandra was admitted to the law program.

The first year of law school is always the hardest. There is so much work that some students buckle under the pressure and give up their studies. Sandra was one of only seven young women in the freshman law class, and she was determined to succeed. The law students would have no idea how well they were doing until after their exams in June, and the atmosphere on campus became tense as the months passed. But Sandra's highly organized schedule kept her a step ahead of many of the other students.

Her quiet self-assurance caught the eye of a fellow student, Beatrice Challis Laws. Sandra's style of dressing, in neat skirts, sweaters, and nylon stockings worn with flat heeled shoes, contrasted totally with Beatrice's casual California look—baggy sweaters, socks, and saddle shoes. But fashion was not the reason they became friends. Although they were very different women, both were diligent about staying in law school. They joined study groups together, discussed legal cases from every angle, and quizzed each other on them.

In the spring of 1950, Sandra enjoyed a double success. She graduated from Stanford *magna cum laude* (with great distinction), as well as completing her first year of law school with excellent grades. Ironically, one of her study partners that year had been William Rehnquist, who was appointed to the Supreme Court in 1972 and is now chief justice of the court on which Sandra Day O'Connor also serves.

The second year of law school was even more competitive than O'Connor's freshman year. Over a hundred students were enrolled in her class. Sandra made friends with people whose paths would later cross her own many times, personally and professionally. Their loyalty would prove valuable to Sandra when she later became a candidate for the Supreme Court.

Some of her happiest times at law school were spent at Cubberley House, where Sandra roomed with her close friends, Beatrice, Catherine Lockridge, Calista Farrell, and seven other female graduate students. This beautiful old house stood at the top of Santa Ynez hill, and lent a certain nobility to the row of fraternity and sorority houses stretching out below. The girls took turns making the evening meals. They felt comfortable enough to invite their dates over for dinner or parties. Sandra went out with a few men, and although she had

31

a steady relationship with one man in particular, she was in no hurry for marriage.

In fact, keeping up with her various classes required the skill of a juggler. Her professors were quite demanding. Their difficult questions in the classroom tested the students' preparation and sharpened their ability to think on their feet. Sandra came to thrive on the daily challenges meted out by her instructors. It prepared her for the courtroom later on, when she became a lawyer. In the meantime, she continued to score high on all her exams.

Her efficiency left her with energy to spare, so she worked on the *Stanford Law Review* in her third and last year of law school. As an editor of this law journal, which was published four times a year, she selected and edited student articles to be published. Although it was hard work, it was a wonderful change of pace from studying. Another editor of the Journal felt the same way. His name was John Jay O'Connor III, a second year law student whose father was a prominent doctor in San Francisco.

The first time Sandra and John got together was the night they were assigned to cite-check an article for the *Stanford Law Review*. Cite-checking means that any time a court decision is mentioned in an article, it had to be checked for accuracy. It could have been a long and laborious evening, but it turned out to be enjoyable instead. Sandra's sense of humor mixed well with John's ready wit. They planned to meet the next day over more law review work. Sandra went back to Cubberley House that same evening and told her girlfriends that she had met someone who was a lot of fun. He had to be if he could elevate cite-checking to the level of recreation!

Sandra and John turned that one evening into forty-six consecutive evenings together. As they got to know each other, they learned about each other's values and interests. Tennis and dancing appealed to both, and they shared an optimistic approach to life. It was steadily becoming apparent to Sandra that John would make a wonderful husband. John was equally enthusiastic about Sandra. He had never known a woman with so much energy and drive.

She invited him to the Lazy B Ranch in Arizona to meet her family, and they all agreed. Although Harry Day didn't see much of a cowboy in his future son-in-law, he was pleased with his daughter's choice. Sandra and John decided to get married at the end of the year, on December 20th, 1952. Sandra would come to rely on John's unwavering support through some of the most intense moments of her life.

When Sandra graduated that spring in 1952, she was third in her class. William Rehnquist was in first place. Along with her academic achievements, Day had her experience on the *Stanford Law Review* and her membership in the Order of the Coif, a national honorary group for top law students, to recommend her to the legal community. With her marriage coming up in December, it seemed as if Sandra had everything going for her. She hardly expected the obstacles that were about to unfairly interfere with her career.

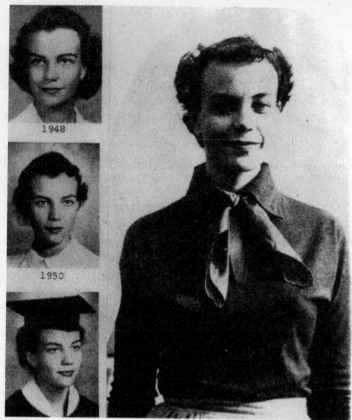

1948

1950

These pictures from Stanford University yearbooks show Sandra Day as a student in 1948 and 1950. Al-though she faced great competition to be admitted to Stanford, her high school academic record was out-standing. In the spring of 1950, Sandra graduated magna cum laude, *and completed her first year of law school as well.*

4

Job Hunt and Marriage

IN THE SUMMER of 1952, Sandra rode the trolley cars all over San Francisco, going from one law firm to the next in search of a job. She went to interviews as far south as Los Angeles, but the law firms were not prepared to hire her. Women lawyers were somewhat of an novelty at the time. Despite Sandra's high academic qualifications, private law firms passed over her just because she wasn't the "right" gender. Finally, she was offered a position as a deputy for the District Attorney of San Mateo County. Grateful for the opportunity to prove herself, she accepted the job. She was also glad to be working near Stanford Law School, where John was finishing his third year.

In the autumn of 1952, Sandra and John began getting ready for their wedding day. Since they had decided to be married on the Lazy B, the Day family was busy preparing for it, too. Alan, Sandra's twelve-year-old brother, and the cowboys spent the better part of a month cleaning up, painting the barn, and doing whatever else they needed to do. It was going to be the biggest event ever held at the ranch.

On December 20, 1952, over a hundred friends gathered in the living room of the Day house. Sandra and John stood before an Episcopalian minister in front of the fireplace and exchanged their marriage vows. Friends came from California, Texas, and farther. Even the Governor of New Mexico, who was an old friend of her father, traveled all the way to the remote ranch for Sandra's wedding.

When the ceremony was over the wedding party moved into a newly built barn for the reception. The strong, clean smell of evergreen wafted out from the pine boughs decorating the rafters. It was a lively, informal celebration. Guests sat on bales of hay, eating Lazy B barbecued beef and listening to the sounds of local musicians. Cowboys mingled with city folk. At the end of the evening, amid a shower of rice, Sandra and John waved good-bye to all their well-wishers and drove to El Paso. There they caught an airplane to Mexico for their honeymoon in Acapulco.

Meanwhile, back at the Lazy B, the celebration continued. It was more than a one-day event. Some friends, who had come a thousand miles, ended up staying a few days. The Day family had worked hard to ready their home for the wedding party, and it had gone off without a hitch and kept going.

The following year, twenty-three-year-old Sandra was promoted to deputy county attorney. She represented San Mateo in civil lawsuits—court cases that

SANDRA DAY O'CONNOR

did not involve criminals. As legal advisor to county
boards, institutions, and agencies, Sandra worked with
the board of supervisors, the school and flood districts,
and the police and fire departments. Her clients, all public officials, were reassured to have Sandra representing them in disputes. She was quick to grasp the numer-
ous laws governing the agencies, and her arguments
showed attention to fine detail.

After graduating from law school the summer of 1953,
her husband, John, found a job in San Francisco, right
over the bridge from San Mateo. The noted criminal
lawyer, Melvin Belli, hired him to do research on a
three-volume work about modern jury trials. Belli was
so impressed with John's work that he asked him to
write portions of the text. However, in October of that
same year, John was drafted. He entered the army as
a private, but in only three months rose to the rank of
first lieutenant in the Judge Advocate General's Corps,
the lawyer's unit in the Army. As assistant Judge Advocate, John gave legal advice on cases dealing with
court-martials—military courts that prosecute soldiers.
His assignment, however, was in Frankfurt, Germany.

As much as Sandra loved working as deputy county
attorney, she was not about to split up their new marriage. She packed her bags and followed John overseas.
Germany was still recovering from the horror of World
War II, which had ended only eight years earlier in
1945. Cities were still devastated, filled with rubble
from bombed buildings. Over three million homes had

37

been destroyed, and most of Germany's factories and railroads still lay in ruins.

After arriving in Frankfurt, Sandra found a job as a lawyer for the Quartermaster Corps or Market Center, which obtained food and supplies—everything from artichokes to armchairs—for the U. S. Armed Forces in Europe. This same unit disposed of millions of dollars worth of surplus equipment to countries as remote as Iceland and Israel. Sandra reviewed the contracts, combing over the fine print to make sure the Army was getting a fair deal. If any claims arose, she took care of them.

When weekends arrived, Sandra and John took full advantage of the time to be with each other. They rented a car and drove wherever they wanted, setting their own pace as they traveled throughout the German countryside. There were wonderful beaches on the North Sea and camping in the Black Forest—so named for the dark, giant fir trees that lined its lush, emerald valleys and surrounded its silvery lakes. Bavaria offered Sandra and John romance, with the spires of fairytale villages set against a backdrop of carefully manicured farms. Rugged, earthy, and jovial, the Bavarian people did their best to make Sandra and John feel right at home.

During John's leave time, they managed to tour fourteen countries in all, from the northern country of Denmark to the warmer southern climate of Greece, and even farther south to Libya, which is in Africa. At the end of John's tour of duty in December of 1956, Sandra and John chose to vacation in the Austrian Alps. They rented a cottage in Kitzbühel, a flourishing little mining town untouched by the ravages of war. Enchanted by the colorfully painted houses and churches, Sandra and John decided to stay for the winter. When they weren't skiing in the Alps, which was just about every day, they went sightseeing throughout the little town. A centuries-old granary, where grain was stored, had been converted into a Tyrolean folk art museum with all the original wood beams still intact. They also toured castles that were almost a thousand years old.

In 1957, as the first buds of spring began to peek through the melting snow, Sandra realized she was pregnant. She and her husband knew it was time to go home to America. They would, however, never forget the enchantment of Kitzbühel, or the hospitality of the German people.

5

Starting a Family

WHEN SANDRA AND John returned to America, they thought about living in California. John's family and most of their Stanford friends resided there. Besides, they were already certified lawyers in California. Since the laws change from state to state, lawyers must pass separate exams to practice in different places. But since California was so large and sprawling, they wondered how effective they could be there. Both Sandra and John had dreams of living in a community where they could help shape what happened to it.

As both the political capital of the state and the business and commercial center, Phoenix, Arizona, seemed like the perfect choice. Phoenix was growing rapidly, but it was not yet bursting at the seams. Sandra and John liked the fact that it was still a small enough city that they could easily get acquainted with their neighbors. They decided to move there, and for the next twenty-five years they enjoyed the Arizona capital's desert bloom.

In the meantime, their first priority was studying for the Arizona legal bar exam. Sandra and John hunted around for bar review courses to help them prepare. Since the only one they found was offered in the city of Tucson, they moved into an apartment there. Across the hall was a fellow by the name of Tom Tobin, a graduate of Princeton Law School who was also enrolled in the bar review course. The three went to class together in the morning and returned home in the afternoon for poolside discussions. They worked hard, quizzing each other on the hundreds of cases they were required to know for the exam. John's wonderful sense of humor lightened the load and made studying a lot easier for all of them. Often, when he told amusing stories, he would take on different dialects. The ability to make people laugh draws people together. It has been one of the important ingredients of Sandra and John's long and successful marriage.

That fall of 1957, Sandra, John, and Tom passed the Arizona bar exam together. Three days after being sworn in, Sandra gave birth to her first son, Scott Hampton O'Connor. John was quick to find a position with the law firm of Fennemore, Craig, von Ammon & Udall in downtown Phoenix.

That same year, Sandra and John bought an acre and a half of land in the northern part of Phoenix, and excitedly drew up plans to build a new home. They were anxious to move out of their small, cramped apartment.

42

When their house was nearly completed, both of them spent their weekends soaking adobe bricks in skim milk before baking them. It was an old Indian recipe for strengthening the brick. Putting the finishing touches on their house was enjoyable to them. Since their family was going to be raised in this house, it was a labor of love.

Their new baby, Scott Hampton, was a constant delight to them, but John O'Connor knew that his wife was eager to return to the work force part-time. He offered to hire someone to help her with young Scott and the housework. When John and she learned that Tom Tobin was back from his European trip, they invited him over for dinner one night. Tom broached the subject of starting his own law firm. He wanted to open two offices, one in Scottsdale with an older lawyer and the other on the West Side of Phoenix in Maryvale. Sandra seemed the ideal person for his second office. She leaped at the opportunity to return to her profession.

In the spring of 1958, the law firm of Tobin & O'Connor was formed. Sandra covered the Maryvale office on the west side of town in the mornings, while Tom was at his Scottsdale location. With the help of a babysitter, Sandra could work until 2 P.M. and then spent the rest of the afternoon with her son, Scott.

Sandra had done a lot of impromptu speaking in high school, many years earlier. Trials demanded that she think quickly on her feet, so she had the chance to sharpen her skills. The courtroom also gave her an opportunity to test her knowledge of the law in a dramatic

43

fashion. Her "audience" was the judge and the jury. It was important to seize their attention at the start of the case. When Sandra stood up and gave her opening statement, everyone listened. It was obvious to all in the courtroom that she came prepared. She was concise and to the point. Judges were amazed. They were used to wordy preambles from other attorneys. At the finish of a trial, Sandra's closing statements were equally stunning because they were precise and brief.

Sandra was only twenty-seven years old, but she had already gained valuable experience in that first year of private practice. With a second child due, she grew weary of the long drive across the city to Maryvale. Her working arrangement with Tom Tobin lasted until the end of 1959, when another attorney took over her job.

After Brian O'Connor's birth in January, 1960, her hands were full with two small boys. Though she had no intention of staying home the rest of her life, she was not one to take her responsibilities for the family lightly. The formative years are the most significant time in any child's life. Her third son, Jay, was born in May of 1962.

Phoenix continued to grow with the arrival of 2,500 new people each month, and John's law firm prospered. After hiring people to help with the children and housework, Sandra directed some of her energy toward civic activities. She began doing volunteer work for the Republican party.

Sandra was following the footsteps of her mother and father when she registered to vote as a Republican. John became active in Republican politics about the same time. From 1960 to 1964, Sandra became involved as a county precinct committee member. Precinct work is the first rung on the ladder of party politics. Most elected government officials launched their careers at this grassroots level. Her efficiency and tirelessness did not go unnoticed.

In 1962, the committee members from all the precincts rewarded Sandra Day O'Connor by electing her to be legislative district chairman. For the next three years O'Connor was in charge of all the precinct committees in her district. It was an important position that brought her to the attention of the state Republican legislators. O'Connor's reputation for hard work soon found all the precinct members voting for her as vice-chairman of the Maricopa County Republican Party. She worked with the chairman to set policy and direction for the party in Arizona.

The year was 1964 and O'Connor delved into Barry Goldwater's campaign for President of the United States on the Republican ticket. Besides juggling family activities and political activism, O'Connor was also asked to chair the Maricopa County Bar Association Lawyer Referral Service from 1960 to 1962. This service, provided by the professional organization of Arizona lawyers, helped people with legal problems find attorneys. Convinced that the referral service could be effective, she held regular meetings with the staff and encouraged them to come up with ideas for improving the service. Under her leadership, the Lawyer Referral

45

Service became an important and dependable organization.

Sandra Day O'Connor also joined a number of committees on the State Bar Association of Arizona. For most people, membership in one was time consuming enough. But O'Connor organized her schedule to allow for involvement in four committees. On the Legal Aid Committee, O'Connor had to think of ways to get more money for groups such as Indian reservations that could not afford legal services. On the Public Relations committee, O'Connor helped provide newspapers, radio, and television with information on how the Bar Association was important to the community, particularly in providing legal help for poor people. O'Connor's efforts on the Committee for Lower Court Reorganization paved the way for a state constitutional amendment to centralize the functions of the court. In some parts of Arizona, justices of the peace could act as judges and decide disputes. Often, a justice of the peace was an ordinary citizen with no legal training. But after passage of the amendment, only lawyers could act as judges.

O'Connor's work on the fourth committee, on Continuing Legal Education, saw her organizing seminars. She brought together legal experts who spoke about changes in the law as well as trends. On all the committees O'Connor joined, improvements had been made. At the end of three years she felt a great sense of accomplishment.

Word spread throughout the county and the state about O'Connor's excellent abilities. Her passion for

46

hard work inspired the people around her also to work hard without complaint. She had a gift for bringing out the best in people. Government agencies vied for her leadership. The Maricopa County Juvenile Detention Home was swift to offer her the title of Chairman. In 1963 and 1964, O'Connor was the driving force behind the development of a new facility to house juvenile delinquents.

Regardless of her community involvement, Sandra always had time for the people who were close to her. An unmarried woman who helped Sandra with her housekeeping became pregnant. Sandra urged her not to leave the O'Connor home. She told the woman that things would work out. It was the kind of understanding the young woman needed at the time. With her spirits lifted, she stayed and helped out at the O'Connor household during her pregnancy. The young woman left shortly before the baby was due, but the difficult period had been made a lot easier knowing that people like Sandra cared about her.

When the youngest of her sons, Jay, reached the age of three and was enrolled in preschool, Sandra thought about resuming her legal career. It was 1965, and the prospect of having one job instead of working as a volunteer on several committees and boards appealed to her. However, Sandra Day O'Connor wanted to be with her sons before and after school, too. She had worked out a fairly successful arrangement with her first partner, Tom Tobin, but most private law firms wanted their

47

employees on the job from early morning to early evening.

Once again, Sandra turned to the government to answer her needs. William Eubank, the chief assistant to the attorney general of Arizona, found her a part-time job in the attorney general's office. Sandra didn't care whether the task was important or not, as long as she could use her knowledge of the law. Once she accepted responsibility, she always followed through with her best efforts.

As assistant to the attorney general, she represented agencies such as the Arizona State Hospital for the mentally ill and the Arizona Children's Hospital, in addition to the welfare department and other state offices and boards. O'Connor kept the institutions aware of the laws that applied to them. When any of her client agencies were sued for any reason, she took up their defense in court.

O'Connor also spoke out for public agencies before the state legislature. Soon, house and senate members knew about her extensive preparation and knowledge. When O'Connor stood before the state lawmakers, her presence was commanding. Her arguments were clear, persuasive, and always to the point.

As her boys grew older, Sandra's part-time job eventually turned into a full-time position. The attorney general challenged O'Connor with some of the toughest cases that came across his desk. Nothing seemed to stump her. She tackled the workload with her usual meticulous thinking, backed up by a seemingly endless supply of energy. Fast-becoming an expert on issues before the state government, her legal opinions were often quoted in newspaper articles.

Although her job was time consuming, she still managed to remain active in the Republican party. She and John worked hard, along with their fellow Republicans, in the elections of 1966. They canvassed neighborhoods, going from door to door, urging people to vote Republican. Their hard work paid off when the Republican Party wrested control of the state legislature from the Democrats. The winning streak for the Republicans ran all the way to the highest office in the state, with the election of Governor John R. Williams.

Three years later, in 1969, the Republicans showed their appreciation for Sandra's loyalty. A vacancy came up in the state senate in Sandra's legislative district. The Republican party thought Sandra Day O'Connor would make an excellent replacement. Sandra was about to become a major force in the elected government of the state of Arizona.

6
The Peaceful Activist

F OR THE FIRST time since Arizona became a state, both houses of the state congress were controlled by the Republican party. Now that the Democrats were out of power, the Republicans were chomping at the bit to change some of the old, outdated laws.

The legislature was in session from January to July, and with the exception of her family, Sandra gave the senate her full attention. The freshman senators who were not acquainted with O'Connor's earlier job as a lobbyist were surprised to meet a woman with so much authority and expertise.

In her first year in office, she contributed more key legislation than any other freshman state senator in the history of Arizona. First, Sandra Day O'Connor turned her attention to Arizona's abortion law. Abortions were prohibited, and it was a felony, or major crime, to perform one. For example, anyone who gave an abortion to a rape victim who had become pregnant could be put in prison for two to five years. As a member of the senate Judiciary Committee, O'Connor voted to repeal the law. Little did she know how this controversial issue would affect her career many years later.

Many Republican senators didn't know whether to call her a conservative or a liberal. On the one hand, her party could count on her for support for the death penalty. They could also rely upon her opposition to both gun control and busing for school integration. But when it came to issues about the family, or a newspaper reporter's right not to divulge the names of people who secretly gave him information, she was quite liberal. O'Connor felt like her father—the less the government interfered, the better. O'Connor's brand of individualism was flexible, however. She was aware that individuals in some groups, such as minorities, women and the poor, required the attention of the government.

Before her first year was up, a tragedy struck in Arizona. A Phoenix grandmother and four children died in a flash flood in the desert because of a foul-up in search and rescue operations. The county sheriff's department had received a call, and they did the best they could to respond to the emergency. But since they did not have the manpower for rescuing people, their response was not effective.

Sandra took the tragedy to heart, and she was the first in the senate to act. She researched the law and found that sheriffs didn't even have the authority, much less the money, to carry out search and rescue operations. O'Connor set to work and devised a plan for emergencies, along with the majority leader in the house, Burton Barr. After meeting with state and local officials, they wrote legislation and saw it become law. O'Connor and Burton Barr gave the people of Arizona a good plan to deal with disasters and save lives.

In 1970, Sandra Day O'Connor's temporary appointment to the state senate expired. In a new election, she campaigned and won against a Democratic candidate, who was also a woman. The Republicans held onto their majority in the house and the senate. O'Connor was so popular that in the next election, two years later, she was again elected by the voters in her district.

Sandra accepted an appointment to chair the State-County Municipal Affairs Committee. Just about all the new laws that affected the state of Arizona were studied and investigated by that committee.

During her first elected term in 1971, Sandra's growing irritation with sexual bias against women surfaced. One law on the books particularly bothered her. Only a husband had the legal right to manage and control the property that he and his wife had bought together. If a man chose to sell the family home, a woman had no say in the matter. In fact, a woman was legally part of the property owned by a man. The history of a husband's legal right to own his wife dates back many centuries to English common law. When the early colonists came to America, they brought with them English law, a legal system dating back to the Anglo-Saxon conquest in 700 A.D., and even earlier, to the Roman occupation of Britain in 100 A.D.

O'Connor's anger at this long-standing injustice motivated her to act. She organized a committee of legislators, lawyers, business people, and women's rights supporters. Together, they re-wrote the property laws so that husbands and wives both shared responsibility. That was only half the battle.

When a proposal is put in front of the legislators, it is called a bill. It does not become a law until after the legislators vote on it. If most of the legislators are in favor of the bill, then it passes and becomes the law of the state. Although Sandra O'Connor had a bill to put before the senate, she still had to get it passed.

Not about to risk defeat, O'Connor devised a plan. She attached her proposal to a different bill, a new one on marriage and divorce. That way, she avoided a lot of opposition. The bill passed, thanks to O'Connor's shrewdness. Women in Arizona then had the legal right to the control of property with their husbands. They were no longer powerless partners in marriages.

On March 22, 1972, the United States Congress passed the Equal Rights Amendment, which made equality between the sexes a constitutional right. To become law, thirty-eight state legislatures also had to pass the ERA. Two days later, Sandra Day O'Connor bravely stood up in the Arizona senate. Her enthusiasm running high, she said the amendment stood "in the tradition of the other great amendments to the Constitution."

Though O'Connor urged her colleagues to support the ERA, most of the other state senators were opposed to it. In fact, in Washington, D.C., Arizona's U.S. senators,

Barry Goldwater and Paul Fannin, were both against its passage. Opposition in both houses in the Arizona state legislature grew stronger. Some of the arguments against the ERA was that it would destroy the family, or force women to become like men.

Although O'Connor tried hard to champion the ERA, she found that she had little support. The Statewide Coalition on the ERA urged O'Connor to have the other senators vote on the amendment, so the public would know which lawmakers were for it and which were against it. O'Connor was afraid that a public vote would make it harder to change people's minds if they were against it.

Instead, in 1974 Sandra Day O'Connor sponsored a senate resolution for a referendum on ratification of the ERA. A referendum would take the issue directly to the people, and let everyone in the state vote on it. However, even that resolution was unsuccessful. In the end, the state of Arizona never supported the Equal Rights Amendment. And by June 30, 1982, the deadline for making the ERA a constitutional amendment, less than two-thirds of the states supported it. It never became law.

Many other issues were calling for O'Connor's attention, however. She also believed that the ERA was not the only way to solve the problem of inequality between men and women. For instance, cases on wage discrimination were being brought before the federal courts, and some of the worst laws discriminating

55

against women existed right in her own state. O'Connor was ready to do something about them.

She proposed legislation to end Arizona's 1913 laws that allowed women to only work eight hours a day. A lot of women held down two jobs to support their families. Instead of protecting women, these bad laws made it even harder for them to make money. However, a lot of senators didn't see it that way. At one point, it looked as though Sandra's bill was a lost cause. But in the final moments, the senate voted to do away with the old-fashioned law.

Regardless of whether or not her colleagues agreed with O'Connor, they respected her for her intelligence and her ability to solve problems. The senators also appreciated that she always listened carefully to arguments opposing her. She would then quickly set about coming up with solutions. Because of her talent for finding agreement among people who had opposite opinions, the other Republican senators encouraged her to become senate majority leader in 1973. She accepted. Sandra Day O'Connor became the first woman in American history to hold that position in a state legislature.

As majority leader, O'Connor was thrust into the eye of the storm, and she thrived on the challenge. She was responsible for seeing that all the bills written by Republican senators made it out of the committees that studied them and were passed into law by the entire senate. It was not her style to force anyone to think the way she did. Instead, her knowledge and her wise words persuaded them. She spent endless hours researching a bill and looking at all the possible results of it on the people of Arizona. The speeches of some of the senators who opposed her were no challenge to O'Connor's arsenal of facts.

It wasn't an easy task to change Sandra O'Connor's mind about something, though. She demanded that the other senators be equally well-prepared if they expected to debate her. Though some of her colleagues were exasperated by her attention to detail, they still admired her. It was not that O'Connor was a nit-picker when she demanded that a comma be inserted into a bill. She knew that if a court was asked to interpret the law, sometimes even bad punctuation could make the difference between right and wrong interpretations.

O'Connor also believed that some people, such as the mentally ill, were too easily forgotten by lawmakers and deserved more attention. She modernized Arizona's old mental health laws so that men and women who were mentally ill and living in hospitals wouldn't have to live there forever. With the new law, these same people were given the possibility of returning to the mainstream of society.

The large Hispanic population in Arizona also found a friend in Sandra Day O'Connor. The migrant workers employed by the farmers were paid very low wages without any health insurance. If they became sick on the job, they had no means of paying for a doctor. Sympathetic to their plight, O'Connor helped pass legislation for workman's compensation. Money was available to help farm workers if they became ill because of their jobs. And O'Connor supported bilingual education—teaching in Spanish as well as English—in Arizona schools. She felt it would make learning easier for many Hispanic children.

Many senators were against allowing students to learn their lessons in Spanish in the schools. They said that English was the language of America, and that only one language should be spoken. But before Americans settled in Arizona, it belonged to the Indians, then the Spaniards, and finally the Spanish-speaking Mexicans. To take their own language away from these people was like asking them to forget their heritage and to pretend they were English Americans. By teaching in both Spanish and English, however, the school system could demonstrate reverence for both cultures. Although Sandra O'Connor bravely championed this cause, her efforts were not successful.

One voice barely audible in state legislatures is the voice of the poor. Because she had grown up with a strong sense of what was fair, O'Connor helped change some of the tax laws so that poor areas of Arizona received as much aid from the government as the rich areas. O'Connor also encouraged a state-funded system of health insurance, known as Medicaid, for poor people. However, the majority of senators defeated the proposal. Arizona became one of the few states without insurance for their poor citizens.

O'Connor also stood alone when she voted against public aid to private schools. Her own involvement as board member of a private school did not change her opinion about what was right under the Constitution. She felt that one of America's most basic principles, upon which this country was founded, is the separation of church and state. She thought that giving tax money to private schools, which are often sponsored by churches, would mean that the state was supporting religion. Despite Sandra's arguments, the majority of Arizona's state senators passed the measure.

O'Connor also incurred the wrath of Phoenix's leading newspaper, the *Arizona Republican,* because she supported a family planning bill in 1973. Sandra felt that the best way to prevent unwanted pregnancies was through educating people about birth control methods. People would be able to make wiser decisions with more information at their disposal.

Once again, Sandra O'Connor felt herself swimming against the current. To religious conservatives, sexual relations are only allowed between married men and women. On the other hand, supporters of family planning believe that ignorance about sex exacts a high price—pregnant teenagers and unwanted babies. Family planning agencies believe that individuals must make their own informed decisions about sex, and that some religious groups should not keep everyone ignorant, or tell everyone what they can or cannot do. As a practical person, O'Connor championed the cause of family planning and birth control, but she found little support from the other senators and she was unable to change the law.

A year later, in April 1974, some of her colleagues

who opposed the right of women to have an abortion were growing more and more vocal about their point of view. They even wanted the U.S. Constitution amended to forbid all abortions. A bill had originated in the Arizona house urging Congress to pass a Human Life Amendment that would protect the rights of the unborn child. No woman in the United States would be able to obtain an abortion, except when her life was endangered. O'Connor consistently stood by her belief that abortion should be legal.

Later that year, she voted against a University of Arizona stadium bond. A rider had been attached to the bill prohibiting the use of state taxes for abortions at the university hospital. Despite O'Connor's opposition, the bill passed. The state supreme court upheld its constitutionality. Although she could not have known it at the time, Sandra Day O'Connor's stand in favor of a woman's right to make her own choice was going to be used against her years later when she went to Washington.

Although Sandra O'Connor was frequently defeated when she stood up for the rights of women, she was able to accomplish a great deal. Family property laws and farm loans had been changed in favor of women. When she spoke before women's groups she urged women to run for public office. In the early 1970s she was way ahead of her time, when she urged women to push for a change in tax laws which would make child care a deductible expense.

In her five years in the state legislature, she never lost

sight of her first priority, her own family. Mustering all her organizing abilities, Sandra balanced her schedule to include shopping trips on the way home or at lunch. On one occasion, when a legislative meeting spilled over into the evening, Sandra excused herself. Her boys were going to camp and she had to make sure everything was packed.

It was also important to Sandra that her sons be active during the summer months. When the legislature was not in session, her family went on vacations together. Trips such as rafting down Idaho's Salmon River challenged their physical stamina.

Her impulse to volunteer was also kept alive during her career in the senate. Sandra organized an internship program for law students, which allowed them to work and learn in the Arizona legislature. As a board member of Arizona's Heard Museum, she became interested in Indian history. She wrote an extensive account of the major accomplishments of Arizona's Indian tribes.

Because the Indians left no written records, it was difficult to know about their lives during the time when they were Arizona's only inhabitants. Through careful research, Sandra discovered that the Indians had enormous respect for the earth. Their medicine, religion, and poetry were very sophisticated. Arizona, the name of the state, comes from the Indian word *Arizonac,* which means "little spring."

Sandra O'Connor's sense of fairness was obvious even during simple events—such as when the Heard Museum held sales of crafts. Hundreds of people

61

showed up for the popular event, Sandra included. Long lines were wrapped around the museum, and people had to wait an hour just to get in. Patiently, Sandra waited along with everyone else, sitting on a camp stool which she brought to give her legs a rest. Despite her position on the museum board, she refused to take special privileges by getting in ahead of the line.

It was this same sense of fairness that also made O'Connor decide not to run for another term in the Arizona senate. She believed that someone else should have a turn to make their contribution to the senate. Despite her defeats on some issues, such as the E.R.A., Spanish education, and birth control, many of her ideas had become law. O'Connor could move on to other things with a feeling of accomplishment.

However, there was one other reason why she chose to leave the senate. As the majority leader, she was in a powerful position. Not much could happen in the state of Arizona that didn't require her support. Everyone wanted to flatter her and praise her, just to get her support. She began to feel that it was an unhealthy atmosphere in which to work. Having lots of power was not her ambition. O'Connor set herself higher goals than that. Since she wanted to continue in public service, she set her sights on being a judge.

7
Old-Fashioned Justice

I N 1974, PHOENIX, Arizona, was witnessing a crime
wave. In fact, that city had the highest crime rate
in the nation. With her term as a state senator over,
Sandra Day O'Connor decided to run for trial judge
in Maricopa County Superior Court. She based her campaign on replacing "fear in our streets with strength in
our courtrooms." Five years as a senator, combined
with her tough stance on law and order, quickly gave
her a lead over her opponent, and she won the election
easily.

As a trial judge, for the next five years she handled
civil cases that dealt with contract violations and medical malpractice suits. Criminal cases were also heard
in her courtroom, with crimes ranging from burglary
and selling drugs, to rape and murder.

O'Connor was a trial judge for the state court, which
is separate from the federal courts. The state court system begins with trial courts, where judges hear criminal
and civil cases. Above the trial courts are the appellate

courts, which handle appeals from the trial courts. If a person charged with a crime feels that he or she didn't get a fair trial, he or she may take the case to an appellate court where judges will examine the trial. Appellate judges don't look at any new evidence. They examine the law that may have been broken and study the way the trial was handled by the trial judge. After careful consideration, appellate judges may decide that the person's trial was unfair and even send the case back for a second trial.

Federal courts follow much the same system, but only deal with federal laws, the U. S. Constitution, and cases involving the federal government. There are ninety-one federal district courts throughout the country. This is considered the trial level for federal cases. Above the district courts are eleven courts of appeal that cover eleven circuits. Each circuit has jurisdiction over three or more states. If someone wants to appeal a decision of the district court, they must take their case to the appeal court in the same district. If they loose their case on appeal, then sometimes they can go to the highest court in the land—the Supreme Court in Washington, D.C.

As a trial judge for the state of Arizona, O'Connor was not afraid to administer old-fashioned justice, which she considered the highest form of compassion. She ran a disciplined courtroom and insisted on good behavior from everyone who attended her trials. Since she spent part of her evenings reading for the cases she would hear the next day, she expected the same preparation from the attorneys who argued before her. On weekends and vacations O'Connor could be found catching up on her legal reading, which kept her abreast of trends in the law.

Word traveled fast among the legal community. Unless a lawyer was well-prepared, he or she did not dare enter Judge O'Connor's courtroom and risk embarrassment. She had no time for attorneys who filed their papers late, conducted sloppy or casual research on their cases, came in with flimsy arguments, or tried to pull the wool over her eyes. O'Connor discouraged delays in both civil and criminal cases. If a lawyer asked her for more time in a case, O'Connor required a thorough explanation in front of the entire court.

When a lawyer had done a bad job of preparing for trial, O'Connor wouldn't hesitate to tell the defendant to find another attorney to serve his or her best interests. Nor would Judge O'Connor allow "backroom" deals—when attorneys make special arrangements for their clients in the privacy of a judges's chambers. All discussions took place in the courtroom in full view of the public.

Judges interpret the law, which is quite different from being a senator who makes the law. As a senator, Sandra had spent hours laboring over the philosophy, the wording, and the exact punctuation of a law that would affect thousands of people's lives. She rarely saw the individuals she represented, except in senate testimony. But in her role as trial judge, she came face to face with people every day and had to decide their fate.

65

Before handing down punishment, O'Connor had to consider a number of things. She had to weigh the evidence presented by the defense and the prosecuting attorneys. She had to decide whether breaking the law had had a bad effect on society. The defendant's life before he or she committed the crime was another consideration. If the defendant had led a respectable life, then one scrape with the law might be looked upon as a "slip."

O'Connor proved to be sensitive and open-minded in many of her rulings. When she handed down a sentence, she always told the defendant her reasons. O'Connor felt defendants were entitled to an understanding of the way a judge thought.

One such case concerned a woman who had been battered repeatedly by her husband. One night, fearing for her life, the woman fought back. She shot and killed her husband. Her attorney said that she had acted in self-defense. The jury was not sympathetic and convicted the woman of murder. O'Connor was convinced the woman had acted to protect herself against further brutality that may have resulted in her own death.

O'Connor spoke out against the verdict, telling the defense attorney that this woman should never have been convicted. After she gave the woman the shortest possible jail term as dictated by law, O'Connor appealed to the governor to commute or reduce the woman's sentence. Her plea of mercy did not fall on deaf ears. The governor gave the woman her freedom after she served a short time in prison.

To a real-estate broker who had written $3,000 in bad checks, Sandra was not so lenient. The defendant, an intelligent, thirty-seven-year-old woman with two very young babies, faced up to ten years for that serious crime. Because she came from a respected Scottsdale family with all the privileges and advantages of the well-to-do, O'Connor felt the woman should have known better. She sentenced her to five to ten years in jail.

Upon hearing the sentence, the woman shrieked, "What about my babies?" O'Connor left the courtroom and went to her chambers—the judge's office—with the woman's screams still echoing through the walls.

Sandra Day O'Connor was always devoted to upholding the law when she was a trial judge, even if it meant not allowing evidence that was necessary to convict someone of murder. In one trial, a defendant was accused of murdering his children by setting fire to them in a trailer. The police had failed to obtain a search warrant when they investigated, so the evidence they had found was illegally obtained. O'Connor was compelled by the law not to allow the evidence. She leaned over the bench to speak to the district attorney, her voice heavy with the burden of her responsibility. "I don't like to do this," she said, "but this is what the law says."

In another case, the scales of justice had been tipped by the prosecution, and O'Connor was quick to right the imbalance. A man had been convicted of murdering another man for $3,300 in a dispute over drugs. Upon learning that important evidence had been held back

67

by the prosecution, O'Connor said the man's trial was unfair. She canceled the verdict and ordered a new trial right away.

When it came to civil disputes, O'Connor was equally swift in her judgments. In one instance, two attorneys tried to divide up forty valuable greyhound dogs that their clients both owned. Valuable court time was being wasted because the lawyers couldn't agree on anything. O'Connor seized on a practical solution, cutting right to the heart of the matter. She took the attorneys aside and asked one of them to come up with two lists of dogs. Both lists were to be of equal value. The other attorney was to pick one of the two lists for his client. The litigation was over in a matter of fifteen minutes.

After working for three years as a trial judge, Sandra Day O'Connor had a reputation for thinking up very new and different ways to punish people for committing a crime. She worked around a defendant's job or financial status when a prison term created more problems than it solved. Jail sentences could be served on weekends sometimes and making someone perform many hours of voluntary community service was another solution. The defendant was allowed to go forward in his life while meeting his obligation to society.

But what of the victim of a crime? It was bad enough that victims were going to have to live with the memory of the violence. In many cases where they were robbed or physically harmed, they also had to bear heavy financial burdens. Society and the courts were starting to become aware of this. As a result of O'Connor's outspoken opinions on this issue, guilty people had to start paying money to their victims so they could rebuild their lives.

O'Connor worked at improving the judicial system in other ways, too. For instance, she became involved in an experiment to provide speedier trials for civil cases. Lawyers were required to shorten the time they normally took to prepare a case. This new approach kept things moving. As a result, the people who were suing each other often came to an agreement outside of court instead of having an expensive, time-consuming trial. This experiment was so successful that Maricopa County expanded the program.

Because she grew up on a ranch, Sandra Day O'Connor never forgot the sense of community she had grown up with. Neighboring ranchers had always helped each other out in good times as well as bad. Sandra continued to search for ways to do something for the community she lived in, even though it was a big city.

She was particularly concerned about senior citizens, so she became chairman of the Senior Citizen's council at the Phoenix Salvation Army from 1975 through 1981. Sandra and others on the council worked hard to have the government build a housing complex for retired people, called Silver Crest. It was an eight-story facility with 126 apartments, a large dining room that served 55,000 hot lunches to seniors every year and delivered 10,000 more to homebound seniors, an activity center for arts and crafts, a pool room, and a library. The people who worked with her on that project never forgot her incredible energy and drive.

Toward the end of her third year as trial judge, the state Republican party had set their sights on O'Connor becoming the next governor of Arizona. Elections were just around the corner. Two Republican candidates had already jumped into the race—Evan Mecham, a car dealer, and Jack London, an insurance man who didn't have a good reputation for dealing with money. Neither of them seemed like the best candidate, and the leaders of the Republican party were afraid that both of them would lose the election—and cause a number of senators to lose too.

The Republican party clearly needed someone strong for the top of the ticket. Unlike the other two candidates, who spoke in fuzzy generalities, Sandra genuinely understood the problems of the state. Also, unlike Mecham and London, she had already contributed effective solutions to some of them. She was considered a popular candidate with an excellent reputation who would surely bring out the party vote.

On the other hand, she was a woman and, even though it was 1977, it was still considered revolutionary for a woman to become the governor of a state. Though O'Connor was not opposed to running for governor, she was cautious. She would only accept the candidacy on the condition that she receive unqualified support from the Republican party's congressional leaders in Wash-

70

ington, D. C.; Senator Barry Goldwater, former U. S. senator Paul Fannin, and Congressman John Rhodes.

She also needed a guarantee that the party would raise enough money for her election campaign, so she wouldn't have to go into debt herself. Lastly, she wanted a first-rate campaign manager to organize an effective campaign. The Republicans squabbled among themselves and took a long time to meet her conditions. After weeks of agonizing about whether she should leave her judgeship and run for governor, O'Connor decided, in the spring of 1978, not to run. The Democrats won the race, electing Bruce Babbitt to take over the helm of the state.

A year later, in 1979, a vacancy became available on the Arizona Court of Appeals when President Carter appointed Mary Schroeder to a federal judgeship on the Ninth Circuit Court of Appeals. Before Carter's administration only eight women had served on federal courts in history. Carter tried to change this by appointing forty-one women to the federal judiciary during his term in office. In four years Carter achieved more for women in this area than all the other previous presidents combined. Governor Babbitt asked O'Connor to take over for Mary Schroeder as an appeals court judge.

At the time, rumors suggested that the governor's decision was politically motivated. If he moved O'Connor into the appeals court, a job that she could not easily leave or return to, he would not have to run against her in an election if she changed her mind and ran for governor. Governor Babbitt denied the rumors, claiming simply that O'Connor was the most qualified person for the job. O'Connor gladly accepted the new position.

The appeals court, made up of nine judges, was run entirely differently from superior court. Instead of just one judge in the courtroom, cases were heard before panels of three judges. Cases that had been previously tried in lower courts were brought before the panels, usually because the losing side wanted another chance to win. One day of the week, Sandra sat with the other two judges on her panel, listening to attorneys argue why the earlier judgements in trial court should be reversed or upheld.

Following the lawyers' arguments, all three judges discussed the pros and cons of a case before arriving at a decision. If all three did not agree, the two that did agree decided the result of the appeal. Each judge took turns writing the opinion for the panel. O'Connor wrote a total of twenty-nine opinions during her eighteen-month stay on that court.

O'Connor was not the kind of judge who pulled her opinions out of thin air. She believed in what lawyers call *stare decisis,* which is Latin for, "Let the decision stand." This means that before a judge makes a decision, he or she must look at all the decisions that other judges made in cases that have the same kind of circumstances. This rule, which comes from England, is the foundation of American law. It helps to make court decisions remain fair and reliable over long periods of time, with many different judges.

O'Connor's decisions in court were also well written

and to the point. Since she once worked at writing the law when she was a senator, she always tried to respect the lawmakers' original intention when she examined a piece of legislation. Sometimes, however, when a law was badly written it was hard to know exactly what the legislators had in mind. Small mistakes could create injustice and confusion. And when people were confused about the law, they went to court.

O'Connor also had criticisms to make of the federal government's appeals courts. She gave a speech about this at a law school in Williamsburg, Virginia, in 1981. She believed that federal courts got involved in cases too often, and she said that state courts should have more responsibility for appeals. Half joking, she pointed out that a federal robe donned by a former state judge did not suddenly make that person more intelligent than he was before. State judges, she said, could protect the constitutional rights of people just as well.

In O'Connor's opinion, federal appeals courts should only hear cases that involve civil rights. But civil rights activists disagreed. They felt that state courts were often prejudiced, especially in certain parts of the United States. Sometimes, judges on state courts were all white men with Anglo-Saxon ancestors. They argued that justice for black people was fine in theory, but didn't really exist. If the federal courts were closed to minorities and the state courts were unfair, what solution would the people have?

In 1979, O'Connor helped to form the National Association of Women Judges (NAWJ). The problems that women justices had were discussed and solutions were proposed. The other purpose of the NAWJ was to actively work toward increasing the number of women judges. At the very first meeting, O'Connor voted along with the other members for a resolution that supported the appointment of a woman to the Supreme Court of the United States. A year later, in 1980, O'Connor helped to organize a women lawyers association for Arizona.

In the summer of that same year, her reputation as an excellent judge spread as far as England. Her praises would be sung by no less than the chief justice of the U. S. Supreme Court, Warren Burger. O'Connor and the chief justice attended a conference on justice in London. When O'Connor discussed English law, the English judges were speechless. They were not prepared for an American who knew so much about their law. O'Connor made quite a favorable impression—so much so that her reputation would travel all the way back across the Atlantic Ocean and straight up Pennsylvania Avenue to the White House.

8

A Woman For All Seasons

IN THE PRESIDENTIAL election of 1980, little more than a third of women voters favored Ronald Reagan while more than half voted for Jimmy Carter. During the election campaign, Reagan's advisers knew that they had to do something to attract more women voters if they wanted to win. Less than four weeks before election day, Reagan announced that if he was elected, women would play an active role in his administration. He also pledged that a woman would fill one of the first vacancies on the Supreme Court of the United States. President Carter had already appointed quite a few women judges, but unfortunately there were no Supreme Court vacancies during his term.

After Reagan moved into the White House, he was slow to keep his promise. Out of four hundred and fifty high government positions, Reagan appointed only forty-five women. Of the forty-one judges appointed, only one was a woman. One highly visible cabinet post, ambassador to the United Nations, was filled by a woman named Jean Kirkpatrick. Women's rights groups were angry and protested loudly that his campaign promise had been hollow.

The pressure was on when, in the spring of 1981, Reagan learned that Chief Justice Potter Stewart was planning to retire that summer. He had served on the Supreme Court for twenty-three years, since his appointment by President Eisenhower in 1958. Reagan had exactly three months to come up with a replacement.

While the President was in the hospital recovering from an assassination attempt, he reminded Attorney General William French Smith and presidential counselor Edwin Meese about his promise to appoint a woman to the nation's highest court. He didn't want just any woman. She had to agree with his conservative principles by supporting law and order and the death penalty. She also had to believe in the family and oppose a woman's right to have an abortion.

Reagan also wanted a "judicial conservative," a judge who would not use the Supreme Court for political action and social change. He felt that the Court should not stray from the exact words used by the men who wrote the Constitution and the Bill of Rights. Conservatives call this "original intent." Liberal justices like Thurgood Marshall and William Brennan believe that the Constitution was not always written clearly, and that, in fact, courts have been challenged over the last two hundred years by the true meaning of many phrases in the Constitution. Also, society has changed

UPI/Bettmann Newsphotos

On the day that President Reagan named Sandra Day O'Connor to the Supreme Court, her family gathered with her at her office in Phoenix. From left to right are her sons Jay and Brian, Sandra and her husband John, and her son Scott. O'Connor's strong belief in the importance of the family as the smallest unit of American society has been amply rewarded by her husband's and sons' support for her career.

a great deal since the Constitution was written. Because of this, many people argue that the words written by the founders of our country in the Bill of Rights must be interpreted according to these new conditions.

For these reasons, these judges are sometimes called "judicial activists." Judicial activists feel the Constitution must adapt and change with society's needs. They also believe that since the states ignore certain individual rights, it is necessary for the high court to guarantee these rights.

Fred Fielding, another White House counselor, joined Attorney General Smith in making a list of names for possible nomination to the Supreme Court. Sandra Day O'Connor's name was brought to the attention of Attorney General Smith by a number of people from her alma mater, Stanford University. One such graduate who helped champion her cause was Supreme Court Justice William Rehnquist. As the most reliable and vocal conservative on the Court, his recommendation meant a great deal. Both Charles Myers, the law dean at Stanford Law School at the time, and William Baxter, a former Stanford professor, told the president's advisors that O'Connor had a brilliant legal mind. Finally, the chief justice of the Supreme Court, Warren Burger, remembered her astounding performance at the Anglo-American exchange in London the summer before.

Two lists of twenty-five names were presented to the president on June 23. The president politely insisted that his aides narrow down the list to the best women candidates. The four that were finally chosen were Sandra Day O'Connor, Cornelia Kennedy, a judge on the Sixth U. S. Circuit Court of Appeals in Michigan, Mary Coleman, chief justice of the Michigan Supreme Court, and Amalya L. Kearse, a judge on the Second Circuit Court of Appeals in New York.

These women were historically not the first to be considered for the Supreme Court, however. A most remarkable woman lawyer of the 1930s, Florence Allen, came to the attention of President Franklin Delano Roosevelt. Allen had been the first woman to serve as justice on a state supreme court, in Ohio. She was clearly a well-qualified candidate for Supreme Court justice, but in the 1930s public opinion wasn't prepared for a woman on the high court.

On June 25, Attorney General Smith phoned O'Connor to invite her to have dinner with him in Washington. He wanted to discuss the Potter Stewart vacancy. Although she was excited—as were her husband and sons—she did not take it for granted that she would be successful. She was not even certain whether she would accept the nomination if it were offered to her. The responsibility of being on the highest court in the land was enormous. As Supreme Court Justice, her decisions would affect the lives of millions of people.

Besides, a move to Washington, D.C. would mean uprooting O'Connor's husband and his law practice. Although her sons were away at college, Phoenix was still their home. Sandra and John would have to sell their house in Paradise Valley and leave the community they loved.

With all of these thoughts swirling around inside her head as she prepared to fly to Washington, she was taken by surprise at her home in Phoenix. Two lawyers from the Attorney General's department, Chief Counselor Kenneth Starr and Assistant Attorney General Jonathan Rose, showed up on Sandra and John's doorstep on June 27 to give her the first interview.

They wanted to know her views on the role of judges and courts in a democratic society. The two lawyers stayed the entire afternoon to listen to O'Connor. Speaking clearly and concisely, Sandra gave them a sampling of her encyclopedic knowledge of federal law. When the day came to a close, the attorneys flew back to Washington with a clear portrait of the woman who stood behind her accomplishments.

On June 29, O'Connor flew to Washington. The next morning, she arose quite early. Breakfast with Attorney General Smith was the first item on her agenda for that day. Her next stop was a two-hour interview with three of President Reagan's most important advisers. She was asked many difficult questions that were deliberately meant to pressure her.

The advisors knew that if Sandra became the nominee she would have to face such questions from newspaper and television reporters, as well as before the Congress. They had to test her to see if she could handle it. She passed the test easily. At the end of the session, the advisors were more tired than O'Connor.

Never in her wildest dreams had Sandra O'Connor imagined being considered for justice of the Supreme

Court. Far from experiencing exhaustion, O'Connor felt renewed. Each obstacle that she overcame gave her more energy. Finally, O'Connor was ready for the next challenge—a meeting with President Reagan.

At 10 A.M. on July 1, she was whisked past the usual squadron of reporters at the White House gates. A few minutes later, she walked into the Oval Office of the President of the United States. With typical forthrightness and easy charm, she acted quickly to ease the tension. She reminded President Reagan of their first meeting ten years earlier, when he was governor of California and she was a state senator in Arizona. They had talked to each other then about their respective bills on state spending cuts. Reagan, responding to her in his own relaxed manner, was quick to remind her that her bill had passed in Arizona, but in California his bill had not.

Both the president and O'Connor relaxed with each other. Reagan couldn't be happier with her point of view on many issues. Politically, she seemed to be almost as conservative as he was. She shared his view that the proper role of the judiciary was not to make new law, but to interpret it.

Besides politics, O'Connor and President Reagan had other things in common. Each confessed their happiest moments were spent on western ranches, riding horses and roping steers. By the end of the forty-five-minute meeting, the President had no doubt that that he had found the ideal person to be a judge on the Supreme Court.

Sandra went home to Arizona to celebrate the Fourth of July weekend with her family in the mountains. Even though she knew her meeting with the President went well, there was still no guarantee that she would be nominated. She thought she bore too close a philosophical resemblance to one justice already on the Supreme Court, fellow conservative and friend, William Rehnquist.

Meanwhile, the White House "leaked" news of O'Connor's nomination to the press. It was a way of testing public opinion before any official announcements were made. If the candidate proved to be unpopular, the President could always withdraw her name without any embarrassment. Despite the objections from extremely conservative Republicans and the Moral Majority, who thought that Sandra O'Connor was in favor of a woman's right to have an abortion, Reagan decided that O'Connor was his best choice.

On the morning of July 7, 1981, Sandra's mother and father and millions of other Americans fixed their eyes on the television as they watched Sandra accept the nomination from President Reagan. Her family couldn't have been prouder. They turned up the volume as Reagan said it was one of his greatest accomplishments to nominate "a woman who met the very high standards of the U.S. Supreme Court . . . a woman for all seasons."

Public reaction was enthusiastically in favor of O'Connor. A nationwide poll at the end of July revealed that ninety-six percent of Americans supported her nomination.

Not everyone, however, was happy about President Reagan's choice. Within hours of his announcement, telegrams poured into the White House. For every one in favor of O'Connor's nomination, ten telegrams were against it. Twenty-one conservative and anti-abortion groups blasted the president. They had helped to elect him to the White House. Now they felt betrayed because Reagan's candidate did not share their strict views.

The memory of O'Connor's pro-ERA/pro-abortion views as a state senator ten years earlier had a bitter taste for these conservative groups. The religious conservatives felt sure that the president had been misled about O'Connor's background, or that Reagan was flagrantly breaking his campaign promises to them.

Reporters from the press and television, like a pack of bloodhounds, sniffed around every nook and cranny for the most obscure details of O'Connor's life. In interview after interview, her friends and colleagues all agreed that Sandra was hardworking and devoted to the legal profession. Her friends also said that, despite O'Connor's brilliant career, her family always came first.

When the press couldn't find anything against O'Connor, the FBI conducted its own investigation. So did the American Bar Association, a professional organization for lawyers. Over three hundred judges, attorneys, and law professors were interviewed on the question of O'Connor's honesty and professional competence. No one turned up anything negative about her.

Meanwhile, Sandra and her family were beginning to tire of being celebrities all of a sudden. Many people think it's wonderful to be famous—until strangers start calling on the phone in the middle of the night. Although O'Connor changed her phone number, her life in Arizona was still too hectic. Finally, she flew to Washington to prepare for the Senate hearings in a quiet out-of-the-way apartment.

Her arrival in the nation's capital was anything but peaceful. An anti-abortion demonstration was in full swing. Reporters doggedly trailed her into elevators. Though O'Connor refused comment on "substantive issues," she never abandoned her good humor. She kept to a calm, steady pace, unmoved by the turmoil.

After two and a half months of intense preparation, the Senate confirmation hearings began amid great publicity. In the committee room, she answered the Senators' questions clearly and honestly. On September 22, 1981, O'Connor received the unanimous approval of the Senate. She gazed out at the Corinthian pillars that ran across the front of the Supreme Court building across from the Senate, and she hoped out loud that, "ten years from now, after I've been across the street and worked for a while, they'll feel glad that they gave me this wonderful vote."

That same night, a candlelight dinner was given at a restaurant in her honor. The host was Senator Strom Thurmond of South Carolina, chairman of the Judiciary Committee that had questioned O'Connor. After dinner, Sandra reflected humorously on what the reaction of some of America's famous presidents—and their wives—might be to the nomination of a woman.

"Thomas Jefferson and James Madison would be turning over in their graves right now," she said. "But let's hope Abigail Adams would be pleased."

For the next week, Sandra's life was filled with celebrations, public and private, formal and informal. The president held a ceremony in the Rose Garden for O'Connor. Beaming with pride, Reagan said, "The nation demands of judges a wisdom that knows no time, has no prejudice and wants no other reward." O'Connor returned his gaze with a calm, steady look of gracious acceptance.

A few days later, on September 25, 1981, in the privacy of the court's conference room, O'Connor placed her right hand on two of her family's Bibles, which her husband held. She was surrounded by her sons, the Reagans, and the Supreme Court justices. Locking eyes with her family's, she repeated the oath "to administer justice without respect to persons and with equal rights to the poor and to the rich."

Five hundred invited guests were waiting for her in the marble and mahogany courtroom where the Supreme Court sits. Judicial proceedings are always filled with ancient traditions. They began with the bailiff, who has the job of maintaining order in the court, crying "Oyez, oyez," which means "hear ye, hear ye."

The eight other Supreme Court justices stood up from the bench. O'Connor was escorted by Chief Justice Warren Burger to her seat. After taking her second oath,

85

"to defend the Constitution of the United States . . .", O'Connor slipped her black judge's robe over her lavender dress and took her place beside her colleagues. The ceremony lasted all of six minutes.

Before O'Connor's appointment, few people outside Arizona had even heard of her. She suddenly went from being unknown to becoming a household word. It was not only a major turning point in O'Connor's life, it was also a milestone in the life of our nation. In less than two weeks the Supreme Court started a new term—and for the first time in history, a woman would have a say in its decisions!

9

Last Stop, The Supreme Court

WITH HER HUSBAND and a rented trailer full
of furniture and belongings, Sandra set
out for the nation's capital. It was three
thousand miles from Arizona to Wash-
ington, but they were both excited about starting new
jobs and meeting new people.

Their first few days in Washington were hectic. In her
new office, Sandra hung her pictures of Arizona, put
beautiful Indian rugs on the floor, and stocked the book-
shelves with her many books on the law. Despite the
new life she was beginning, some loyal friends provided
a link with the past. For instance, Sandra's secretary in
Phoenix also made the trek across country to continue
working for her. Sandra was grateful for her devotion.
Three law clerks—young lawyers who act as assistants
to judges—of former Justice Potter Stewart also agreed
to stay on. Another law clerk from her husband's Phoenix law firm willingly accepted an opportunity to work
for Sandra Day O'Connor.

O'Connor spent the first week in conference with the rest of her fellow justices, sifting through thousands of appeals that had arrived at the Court since June. Because there is only so much time in each term, it was important that they chose only the most important ones. They finally decided to hear less than two hundred cases that term.

Hundreds of people lined up for Sandra Day O'Connor's historic first day on the Court, October 5, 1981. After everyone was seated, the justices emerged. They wore long black robes and took their place at the long, high table that allowed them to look out over the courtroom.

Attorneys were given thirty minutes to argue their cases. O'Connor quickly set the tone for her newest job. When she encountered a lawyer's murky reasoning or interpretation of the law, she did not hesitate to speak up and ask tough questions. The other judges, as well as people watching, were impressed by her command of the new situation. At the end of the first session, all the justices left the courtroom for their chambers. Stacks of paperwork waited on their desks.

Each Friday, the justices held conferences. No one else was permitted to attend these secret meetings, where the cases they'd heard the previous Monday were discussed. Each justice had to give his opinion on how the case should be decided. Because O'Connor was the newest judge, by tradition she had to answer the door and take messages. After a vote was taken, the chief justice, if siding with the majority, then assigned a justice to write the majority opinion. If the chief justice voted with the minority, then the most senior associate justice would assign the opinion. The minority justices agreed among themselves who should write the dissenting opinion.

When these opinions were written, all the judges read them. During this time, they could still change their minds. Sometimes the dissenting opinion might become the majority opinion. Other times, a Justice who voted with the majority did not necessarily agree with how the majority arrived at its opinion. In that case, the Justice wrote his or her own opinion, called a concurrence, to reflect their exact views on a case. Although Sandra O'Connor sided with her conservative fellow justices, Burger and Rehnquist, on many majority opinions, she did not hesitate to write her own separate opinions. She was very much her own person.

By December of 1981, the welcoming parties were finally over. Sandra's workload increased. She got up each day well before dawn to catch up on some of her reading of briefs. By 6:30 A.M. she was already at an exercise class. An hour later she was in her chambers, where she often stayed as late as 8:30 P.M. Her devotion to being well prepared meant that she worked even on Saturday at the courthouse. Out of this relentless schedule, Sandra managed to carve a block of time for recreation. On Sundays she gardened and golfed. Cooking, dancing, and volunteering were luxuries for which she could no longer afford the time. However, Sandra did have time for her family. She went home to Arizona for

89

Thanksgiving and Christmas. She even managed to squeeze in her class reunion at Stanford and a trip to Africa after the Court recessed that first year.

After O'Connor's first year on the Supreme Court it was obvious that she was a judge who made up her own mind. The Court had become more conservative compared to the previous Court, but each of the other justices, like O'Connor, held definite opinions about the law. With so many different opinions, the Court was always agreeing to disagree. A lot of decisions, when five judges voted one way and four voted the other way, made for spicy conflicts. When a conservative such as O'Connor arrived on the scene, the tension was pitched to a new high. Her independence irritated some of the older Justices and challenged the thinking of her liberal colleagues.

O'Connor may have sided with conservative Justice Rehnquist most of the time, but she veered sharply from his judicial activism. O'Connor held onto her belief in *stare decisis*. She took great pains not to overturn precedents. A good example was a discrimination case that came before the Court in that first term. O'Connor felt the defendant had not done all he could at the state level before turning to the highest court in the land. But the Supreme Court had already ruled in 1978 that a defendant in a similar case did not have to exhaust state "remedies" before going to the Supreme Court. Reluctantly, O'Connor voted with the majority. She was firm about not disturbing a earlier decision of the Court, even if that same decision went against what she personally believed to be a sound policy.

She was also careful not to intrude upon the legislative branch of the government. The lawmakers, as representatives of the majority of the people, ought to make and refine the law, O'Connor believed. The less the judiciary interfered with correcting legislative mistakes, the better. To the liberal minority on the Supreme Court, however, the Court was the most effective guardian of an individual's rights against majority rule.

True to O'Connor's background in state government, she also continued to pursue federalism in the high court. Her fervor, as always, was based on reasoned analysis: the original framers of the Constitution, our very first lawmakers, set up a clear boundary between the authority of the federal government and the independence of the states. One case that challenged the power of the state stands out for all its romance and history.

It involved a sunken treasure. A Spanish ship by the name of *Nuestra Senora de Atocha,* had gone down off the coast of Florida in 1622. The Spaniards were sailing back to Spain from the New World. The ship was filled with all the treasures taken from the colonies. Forty miles into their trip home, a hurricane raged across their path, and in moments the *Nuestra Senora* sank along with all the gold and other priceless treasures destined for King Philip IV of Spain. Nearly three hundred and thirty years later, in the 1950s, a company was formed to hunt for treasures on the bottom of the ocean. The group, known as Treasure Salvors, systematically combed through old Spanish shipping records to pinpoint the exact location of the *Nuestra Senora*. After twenty years of searching the ocean, they found their treasured wreck in 1971. Millions of dollars in gold and other valuables were lying in the ship. Their hard-earned efforts finally paid off.

Then the state of Florida stepped in, claiming they owned the treasures because the ship had gone down on "state-owned submerged lands." Both Florida and Treasure Salvors vowed to fight it out in court. At one point, Florida took possession of part of the gold. By the time the case finally reached the Supreme Court, it was very complicated. Did the federal government have the right to seize control of state property? To complicate matters further, there was the question of Florida's sea boundaries. The Supreme Court finally ruled the Spanish galleon was outside Florida's boundaries. Treasure Salvors reclaimed their riches ten years after first discovering the sunken *Nuestra Senora de Atocha*. Though O'Connor voted along with the majority decision, she disagreed with some of the ruling. Her convictions on federalism proved to be intact: she did not like the federal government interfering in disputes between a state and one of its citizens.

It was only the beginning of her new job, but Sandra Day O'Connor was already very strong on the Court. In her opinions, she favored the government over the individual. This stands in bold opposition to her long-held belief that the individual is the cornerstone of society.

The liberals on the Court felt O'Connor, along with the other conservatives, had tipped the scales of justice in favor of the police, prosecutors, and state judges at the expense of the defendants. But O'Connor argued that innocent people must be protected from people who break the law, and the people who protect us from criminals should not be hampered in maintaining order in society.

But if the conservative justices thought they could relax, with the comforting notion that O'Connor was always on their side, they were wrong. She astonished everyone by voting liberally when it came to sex discrimination.

In one case, a man had been denied admission to Mississippi University's all-female nursing school. He sued on the grounds that he was discriminated against because of gender. In writing the majority opinion, O'Connor could find no good reason for the state university to keep men out. She wrote that the policy reflected old-fashioned ideas that only women should be nurses. Therefore, she concluded, the school violated the Fourteenth Amendment, which protected the man's freedom to attend a public institution. A close parallel existed in an old case involving discrimination. O'Connor reminded her fellow justices of that decision from 1873.

At that time, the Supreme Court had unanimously agreed that women could not be lawyers due to their "peculiar characteristics, destiny and mission." States had been given the power to keep women out of the legal profession because those "energies and responsibilities" were best left to the "sterner sex." Today, everyone knows this is nonsense.

Sometimes, even when Sandra joined the liberals in deciding cases of sexual descrimination, her reasons differed from theirs. Women complained that a club called the Jaycees had only men as members. The majority of judges agreed that this was discrimination. They said that admitting women to the club wouldn't violate the group's message of personal and professional development. However, O'Connor believed the real issue was whether the group was a commercial club or not. If it was commercial, a place where business deals were made, then the state had the right to make laws about the membership because the state can control commerce.

In one case, O'Connor came down heavily on a law firm that discriminated against women attorneys. The attorney for the law firm claimed that the laws against discrimination didn't apply to law firms. He claimed that Congress "intended" it that way. Her patience strained, O'Connor told the defense attorney that Congress was quite capable of writing exceptions to the law when they chose to. But since they hadn't in this case, the Supreme Court was being asked to create an exception. In short order, the majority of the judges on the Supreme Court ruled in favor of the woman attorney.

But O'Connor didn't look at every sex discrimination

case the same way. In the case of *Ford Motor Company* v. *Equal Employment Opportunity Commission,* three women claimed that Ford's hiring practices discriminated against them. They had applied for a warehouse job, but men were hired instead. Women had never before worked at that job in all of Ford's history.

O'Connor, writing for the majority, said that Ford had been discriminatory. But O'Connor also wrote that all Ford had to do to correct the situation was to offer jobs to the women. She said that Ford did not have to make up for discrimination that took place years earlier. Feminists condemned O'Connor for her decision. They felt O'Connor owed it to all women to use her power to rule in their favor. O'Connor disagreed. Each case had to be evaluated by its own facts.

In her second term, a number of cases on abortion came before the Court. Only ten years earlier in 1973, the Court had decided that a woman's choice to have an abortion was a right protected by the Constitution. The name of that famous case was *Roe* v. *Wade.* The majority ruled that local regulations that made abortions difficult for women to obtain were unconstitutional. While her loyalty to *stare decisis* prevented her from changing a previous ruling of the Supreme Court, the reasoning behind *Roe* v. *Wade* annoyed Justice O'Connor.

Roe v. *Wade* held that the state could not interfere with a woman's privacy in the first trimester of pregnancy. (A trimester is three months). The Court chose the trimester because during this time a fetus cannot

95

survive outside the womb. With new medical technology, however, some people claimed that a fetus could survive outside the womb at a later stage. In a 1983 case on abortion, the majority of judges upheld *Roe* v. *Wade,* but Sandra Day O'Connor disagreed. In a dissenting opinion, she reasoned that "at any stage in pregnancy there is the potential for human life."

O'Connor disliked the fact that the Supreme Court was being called upon to act as a kind of medical board. She believed court rulings should be based only on the Constitution, an impartial document, rather than medical technology, which is constantly changing. As medicine advances, a woman can have safe abortions well into the second trimester of pregnancy. However, because of the same medical advances, a doctor can help a fetus live outside a woman's body at an earlier stage of its development. O'Connor felt that the trimester approach which had been set out in *Roe* v. *Wade* in 1973 was a problem. The whole issue was, as she put it, "clearly on a collision course with itself."

O'Connor thought that the lawmakers in Congress, not judges, should make the kinds of changes that she felt were needed. While the anti-abortionists who had opposed her nomination were now very happy about O'Connor's views, feminists were not. With O'Connor's careful, well-thought out dissent, the groundwork for changing the decision in *Roe* v. *Wade* was in place. However, when another abortion case came before the court seven years later, O'Connor would startle the other justices with a perspective on abortion that seemed at odds with her opinion in 1983.

Media watchers kept a close watch on O'Connor's third term, in 1983–84. The presidential election was coming up in November. Reagan's re-election would mean the appointment of one or two justices in line with his conservative point of view. Already, the Supreme Court was becoming more and more conservative. In her third term, O'Connor had sided with the conservative Justices Burger, Rehnquist, White, and Powell nine times. Only once had she sided with the liberal coalition of Justices Brennan, Marshall, and Stevens. Decisions made by the liberal Warren Court years earlier were in danger of being changed.

In that same term, another important guarantee from our Bill of Rights was challenged—the Fifth Amendment's protection against self-incrimination. In 1966, the liberal majority had ruled in *Miranda* v. *Arizona* that police had to read a suspect's rights to him before questioning him. A suspect had the right to remain silent and the right to have a lawyer present. This became known as Miranda rights.

In 1984, a man named Benjamin Quarles challenged the Miranda ruling. He had been charged with the crime of possessing a weapon. Since he matched the description of a rape suspect, police apprehended him, frisked him, and discovered an empty shoulder holster. They asked him where the gun was. After Quarles told them where it was, they found it. Before questioning him any further, the police read him his Miranda rights. Because

97

they had not given him the warnings earlier, a lower court ruled that Quarles' confession and the gun could not be used as evidence in court.

Justice Rehnquist, who wrote the opinion for the majority, said police could dispense with the warnings if they felt instinctively threatened. But O'Connor stood by her conviction that judges should not tamper with previous laws. The *Miranda* case had balanced individual rights against effective law enforcement. Now Justice Rehnquist wanted to make an exception to the rule. O'Connor felt that he was chipping away at a clear and reasonable law.

In the end, she agreed partly with the majority, but she made a distinction. Evidence obtained as a result of the police merely failing to give Miranda rights could be used in court, but evidence that the police had received because they forced a suspect to speak and violated *Miranda,* could not be used in court.

O'Connor also joined the conservative majority in limiting the rights of prisoners. The Fourth Amendment protects people from being searched or arrested unless the police have a good reason. However, the Court denied a prisoner's claim that he still had rights to privacy in his prison cell. O'Connor was more concerned with the safety of the prison guards than the prisoner's rights.

In such cases, Sandra O'Connor clearly favored the conservative point of view. She agreed with another Court decision that allowed illegal evidence to be used in court if the police had seized it in "good faith." In other words, Fourth Amendment violations were all right as long as the police didn't mean to be bad.

One of the saddest cases to come before the Supreme Court in O'Connor's third term was a shoot-to-kill case called *Tennessee* v. *Garner.* One night, a Memphis policeman was called to the scene of a burglary of a vacant building. When the officer arrived, he saw a fifteen-year-old boy running from the back of a building and crouching near a fence. Though the officer told the boy to halt, the boy started to climb over the fence to escape. The officer shot him with his revolver. In a matter of moments the boy was dead.

The Memphis police officer admitted the boy was unarmed and hadn't hurt anyone. During questioning, Justice Stevens found out that running away from the police is not even a crime under Tennessee law—it's only a minor offense against a city law, punishable with a $50 fine. The officer's attorney, however, claimed the Tennessee law was "shoot-to-kill."

A brilliant attorney argued for the suspect's survivors. He contended that someone running away from the scene of a crime should be shot only if the officer believed the suspect was likely to violently harm someone. The lawyer showed the Court studies which proved crime rates did not go down because of shoot-to-kill policies. In fact, police officers all over the country had filed briefs with the Supreme Court saying that shoot-to-kill policies often ended up with policemen being shot instead of criminals.

A majority on the Court ruled that the Tennessee law

was unconstitutional. O'Connor disagreed, along with Burger and Rehnquist. The boy had stolen only ten dollars and a purse. But the three dissenting justices felt the young boy chose to risk his life by fleeing. They believed the need to prevent crime is greater than the individual's interest in his own life. O'Connor criticized the majority who found the Tennessee law constitutional, claiming that it would make the police's job even more difficult. Once again, Sandra O'Connor favored the government over the rights of the individual.

10
A Voice for the Future

I N 1984, RONALD Reagan was elected to a second
term as president of the United States. He wanted
the Supreme Court to get tough on crime. He urged
them to change the rulings of the liberal Warren
Court of the 1960s. Ironically, this meant the Court
would have to become an activist Court, which was exactly what conservatives complained of when they criticized the Warren Court. Reagan's position smacked of
hypocrisy.

Edwin Meese, an old friend and adviser of the president's, became the attorney general. He was in charge
of all the government's lawyers at the Justice Department. Both Reagan and Meese believed that the 1960s
and 1970s were periods of great leniency toward people
who were suspected of committing crimes. Some lawyers looked upon Edwin Meese, a former prosecutor
from Oakland, California, as a "cheerleader" for the police. Constitutional rights were often viewed by Ed
Meese as annoying difficulties that stood in the way of

criminal convictions. He especially hated the *Miranda* ruling. Despite his tough stand on law and order, in 1987 Edwin Meese was forced to leave his job as attorney general, because he had broken ethical standards while in office.

The Reagan administration didn't like it when people used the courts to get rid of political and economic inequality. Liberal activists, often defeated at the polls, were frequently victorious in the federal courts. The Justice Department, working hand in hand with the president, wanted to stop this. However, the judges of the Supreme Court remained independent, and refused to blindly obey the President.

Five years had passed since President Reagan had appointed Sandra Day O'Connor. While she leaned to the right on many cases, she also had rejected the views of the Reagan administration on issues. She was especially against the Justice Department's efforts to prevent mental patients from suing to obtain disability benefits.

In one of the biggest defeats for the President, the Court overturned a 1965 decision that allowed prosecutors to exclude blacks from juries, simply because they might favor defendants of their race. In another victory for minorities, the Court ruled that if a defendant had been convicted by a grand jury from which members of his race had been illegally excluded, the conviction must be thrown out.

The administration lost again when the Supreme Court ruled on a case called *Maine* v. *Moulton.* Statements that a defendant gave to a police informer with a hidden transmitter could not be used to convict the defendant. It was just too much of a setup to be considered legal.

However, the Supreme Court agreed with the administration's desire to limit a suspect's Miranda rights. In *Moran* v. *Burbine,* the police deliberately kept information from both the suspect and the attorney representing him. While police officers interrogated the suspect, the police did not tell him that his attorney had been trying to reach him. O'Connor's majority opinion said that as long as police told suspects of their Miranda rights to remain silent and to have a lawyer present, they didn't have to do anything else. It didn't matter even if the suspect's lawyer was trying to contact him.

Justice Brennan angrily disagreed with O'Connor and the rest of the majority. He felt that *Miranda* had been dealt a "crippling blow." He saw this as part of the "disturbing trend" toward weakening our Bill of Rights. He accused the conservative justices of helping prosecutors convict defendants without regard to their constitutional rights. "One can only hope that this day too will soon pass," wrote Justice Brennan.

Soon the conservative wing of the Court grew even stronger. Reagan appointed two new judges, Antonin Scalia in 1986 and Anthony Kennedy in 1988, to replace two retiring judges, Lewis Powell and Warren Burger. The liberals were now in the minority. Rehnquist became chief justice. Rights such as freedom of speech and religion, as well as protection from unreasonable

103

police searches and seizures, were challenged regularly in his court.

One of the most surprising decisions of the Rehnquist Court was a majority opinion in the 1988–89 term. The Supreme Court decided that burning the American flag was an exercise of free speech. A man named Gregory Lee Johnson had protested Reagan's nomination for reelection at the 1984 Republican National Convention in Dallas, Texas, by setting the stars and stripes on fire. This was against the law in Texas, and Johnson was convicted of the crime. He appealed, he said, because the law took away his First Amendment right to freedom of speech. This time the conservative Justices Scalia and Kennedy surprised the rest of the Court by joining liberal Justices Brennan, Marshall, and Blackmun. Together they upheld Johnson's right to communicate freely.

Like Justices Rehnquist and White, however, Sandra O'Connor disagreed. She didn't think that burning the flag in public was necessary to express an opinion, and she also felt that it might created a violent situation. This became a very emotional issue. Reagan's successor, President George Bush, who had been elected in 1988, campaigned for an amendment to the Constitution that would outlaw flag burning. He didn't get the constitutional amendment, but he convinced Congress to pass a new law against flag burning.

In 1989, in a case called *Webster* v. *Reproductive Health Services,* a woman's right to have an abortion was under fire again in the Supreme Court. *Roe* v.

104

Wade, which held that American women have a constitutional right to make their own decision, was in danger of being overturned. In *Webster* v. *Reproductive Health Services,* the Supreme Court upheld a Missouri law that prohibited state money for abortions except where the mother's life is in danger. The decision created a broad exception to *Roe* v. *Wade,* and allowed state governments to pass laws which severely limit a woman's right to choose.

Justices Rehnquist, Kennedy, White, and Scalia adopted the reasoning so carefully put forward seven years earlier by Sandra O'Connor, in 1983. They said that the government's interest in potential life should run the entire length of the pregnancy. Therefore, they said that the trimester approach, which was used in *Roe* v. *Wade,* should be scrapped. Four other judges argued against this. Sandra O'Connor held the key vote.

Although O'Connor sided with Rehnquist, Kennedy, White and Scalia—forming the majority opinion—she remained strangely silent about her earlier thinking on the trimester approach in her 1983 dissenting opinion. O'Connor declared that the Missouri law did not question the legality of abortions, but merely whether or not states could place restrictions on them. One of the main principles of the Court, she pointed out, is not to rule on a matter that is not specifically under consideration. Therefore, O'Connor reasoned, the Court did not have to decide if *Roe* v. *Wade* had been correctly decided in 1973.

O'Connor's position angered fellow Justice Scalia, for

National Historical Society

In this official portrait, the nine Supreme Court judges are, from left to right, Thurgood Marshall, Antonin Scalia, William J. Brennan, Jr., John Paul Stevens, Chief William H. Rehnquist, Sandra Day O'Connor, Byron White, Anthony M. Kennedy, and Harry A. Blackmun. With the appointments of Scalia in 1986 and Kennedy in 1988, President Reagan finally tilted the court's balance from liberal to conservative.

if she had followed her original reasoning, the Court may have been able to overturn *Roe* v. *Wade*. He criticized O'Connor's stand strongly and said it was not a serious position. He even went so far as to call it "perverse" and "irrational." In the end, the only thing the five Justices in the majority agreed on was that state governments did not have to pay for poor women to have abortions, and did not have to allow abortions in public hospitals. Standing firmly on the principle of *stare decisis* again, Sandra O'Connor wrote that *Roe* v. *Wade* should not be overruled—at least, not yet.

Usually conservative Justices are very strict about heeding precedent. The liberal Justices often give the Constitution a broader meaning. Yet in this instance, it was the conservatives—who are opposed to a woman's right to have an abortion—who tried to give the law a wider interpretation. While O'Connor may have seemed liberal to Scalia in the sense that she did not strike down *Roe* v. *Wade,* she was actually acting in a very conservative manner. As it stands today, three Supreme Court Justices want to change the Roe decision to give governments more power. Justice Scalia wants to overthrow it completely.

The Supreme Court's decision on the Missouri statute may have done more to strengthen abortion rights. The decision has had unexpected consequences everywhere. In Missouri, for example, public hospitals stopped performing abortions. At one state college, the staff were told not to give anyone any information on abortions. Other state employees were also forbidden to discuss the topic. Despite this, almost all of the private clinics in Missouri still offer abortions, and the government has no right to stop them. The people most affected by the Supreme Court's decision are poor women, who cannot afford to pay for their abortions.

Since *Roe* v. *Wade* gave women the constitutional right to an abortion, that right has been taken for granted. With the most recent Court ruling, it suddenly seemed that women might lose that right. The women's movement came back to life, demanding that women be allowed to make their own choice. A dramatic political change began to occur as well. All over the country voters reacted angrily against the idea of the government telling people what to do in their private lives.

In some state elections, anti-abortion law makers were voted out from office and replaced by pro-choice candidates. Political victories were also won in state legislatures, which relaxed restrictions on funding abortions. A major political shift in favor of abortion rights saw California voters install pro-choice Republicans for state senators. In November, 1989, a black man, L. Douglas Wilder, was elected governor for the first time in the history of Virginia. It was a narrow victory, but Wilder's opinion that women have a right to choose gave him the lead over his conservative opponent.

Other cases on abortion are still coming before the Supreme Court. An Ohio law requires that teenage girls tell one parent or obtain permission from a judge in order to get an abortion. Another law in Minnesota says that teenagers must have the permission of both of their parents—even if one of the parents has left home. Sandra Day O'Connor is skeptical about the Minnesota law, because it doesn't provide for any exceptions. Often, children are raised by only one parent, and their other parent is not a part of their lives. O'Connor does not believe a teenage girl should be forced to have an unwanted baby because she can't get permission from a parent absent from her life.

A third abortion case is coming to the Supreme Court from Illinois. There, the legislators passed a law that created very high standards for private abortion clinics. Because of this, many have been forced to close. People who are in favor of a woman's right to choose claim that the standards are too high and were only created to make problems for the clinics and force them to close.

Sandra Day O'Connor insists that a law should be struck down if it puts "undue burden" on a woman's right to an abortion—if the law makes it much too hard for a woman to choose. But O'Connor has not yet said what she thinks "undue burden" means. If O'Connor decides that the Minnesota law restricting abortions to minors is unconstitutional, she will be declaring that the 1973 *Roe* v. *Wade* ruling is valid. She will also be forced to shed some light on her true views on abortion.

Besides abortion, O'Connor has also run into opposition from her conservative colleague, Justice Anthony M. Kennedy, on the issue of religion. In a democratic country, the government must be completely separated from all religions and churches. Governments are not allowed to support a religion in any way.

In one case, O'Connor said that cities could not display a Christmas manger scene on the main stairwell of City Hall. This display, she said, showed support for a certain religion. Justice Kennedy called her decision "bizarre."

In spite of their attacks on each other, the conservative judges still find much in common when it comes to civil rights. African–American leaders accuse them of being against civil rights for minority races. For instance, the Supreme Court overturned a decision of the city council of Richmond, Virginia, which set aside 30 percent of its contracts for minority businesses. In the most recent term of 1989–90, the Court decided not to hear a single civil rights case.

Many important cases will be heard, however. The Supreme Court has yet to rule on what some people call the "right to die." A woman named Nancy Beth Cruzan has been in a coma since 1983. Doctors say she will never be conscious again, and they keep her alive with machines. Her parents want to let Nancy's body die.

The Cruzan's did not have any kind of written permission from Nancy to let her die if she ended up in that condition. The state of Missouri said that written permission is necessary. Without it, Nancy Beth's body will have to lie in a hospital bed for many years to come. The state government has blocked the Cruzan family's wishes to let their daughter die.

This is one of the most important cases to come to the Supreme Court in a long time, and whatever the Court decides will affect the lives—and deaths—of

Americans for many decades into the future. Conservative members of the Supreme Court do not feel that the Constitution gives people the right to die. O'Connor favors a ruling that balances the interests of the parents and the state.

Almost a decade has passed since O'Connor became the first woman to sit on the United States Supreme Court. Having measured up to the challenge, she looks forward to many more years as a justice. She has weathered the demanding work schedule and written her share of majority opinions, as well as her own separate concurrences to shed clarity on an exact point.

Sandra O'Connor's life has flourished because she has always been able to balance work and recreation. Doing exercises each morning gives her energy. A game of golf, and gardening on Sundays, as well as her regular social appearances, give her breaks from her heavy schedule. Her husband has always given her tremendous support for everything she has done. And recently, Sandra has become a grandmother with the arrival of her son's new baby. Though her mother and father died toward the end of the 1980s, Sandra still maintains close ties to her brother and sister.

Although Sandra O'Connor has always maintained that her own private opinions do not influence her judicial opinions, judges are still human. A person's intellect and emotions do not develop separately. They are shaped by the family you grow up in, school, and career. Sandra came from a privileged background. Both her parents were bright, supportive people. While her fam-

111

ily was not rich, they had enough resources to send her
to a private girls school and later to a private university.

As a result, Sandra O'Connor's opinions are those of
a successful, hardworking woman who seized the opportunities she found open to her. But greatness is also
the ability to feel for those who are less privileged—and
O'Connor has shown over and over again that she will
stand up for the poor and the ignorant.

Everyone agrees that Sandra Day O'Connor is not a
token female justice. Hard work and her performance
in the court have proven that. Her swift, no-nonsense
attitude and her tough law-and-order opinions in criminal matters are often seen as "masculine" in this cul-
ture. But, in fact, all women and men have some of the
characteristics of the opposite sex inside them.

Sandra O'Connor's upbringing on a ranch nourished
both sides of her personality. She played with dolls, but
she also did the same things a young boy would normally do—drive a tractor, ride horses, and repair
fences. Consequently, she managed just as easily as a
mother raising her sons as she did as an attorney fighting in court. Her role models—her grandmother and her
parents—were strong and independent. Because her intelligence and ambitions were encouraged, Sandra
grew up feeling that she could do whatever she wanted
to with her life.

Intelligence, hard work, and persistence—these characteristics allowed her to rise above any difficulty she
might have had just because of her gender.

The key to her life is to never look back. After she

considers all sides of an issue, Sandra O'Connor makes up her mind and sticks to it. Despite opposition from her fellow justices and the public, she fearlessly stands by her decisions. Although she doesn't always agree with the women's movement on all issues, she's an excellent role model for women everywhere. She has balanced her desire to have a family with her career. She focused on immediate goals. Whatever the task at hand, she did it well. This not only gave her a sense of fulfillment and was appreciated by the people around her, but it was the door to new opportunities.

Her sense of fairness has raised the ethical standards of the legal profession. Her valuable contributions to the law are causing men to respect women in the legal profession. She has held some of the most powerful positions in both state and federal government. But throughout her careers, she has never lost sight of the importance of her own family. Sandra Day O'Connor has paved the way for women who will follow after her.

A few years after she was appointed to the United States Supreme Court, Sandra Day O'Connor described the simple personal philosophy that has inspired her to work so hard for her state and her country. All people, she said, "are here on earth for a very short time. As stewards of this planet, we need to make sure that we don't damage it. And if we can, we must leave it better than when we came."

113

APPENDIX

A VIEW FROM THE BENCH
How the Supreme Court Works

THE UNITED STATES Supreme Court is the highest court in the country. Its chief responsibility is to determine whether or not federal, state, and local governments are acting according to the United States Constitution. This is often not as simple as it may appear. When the Founding Fathers wrote the Constitution in 1789, they couldn't possibly predict what the modern world would be like two hundred years later. Problems arise today that the Founding Fathers never even thought of.

Over the years, the Supreme Court has changed in a number of ways. Just after the American Revolution, the Court was founded to help the states work out their economic difficulties. Under the Articles of Confederation of 1781, each state acted on its own behalf. To raise money, states on the coast would place high tariffs on products travelling from the sea to inland states. This caused conflicts and tension between the states. It became necessary to create an institution to solve these problems. When the Constitution was written in 1789 and more power was transferred to the central government, Article III provided for a federal judiciary system that would include a Supreme Court and lower courts.

The power the judiciary branch has to affect the law is kept in balance by the two other branches of the government: the executive branch and Congress. The executive branch—the President—has the power to appoint new justices as the old ones retire or die. Thus, he or she can attempt to control the political beliefs of the Court. However, the President's choices must be approved by the Senate. And Congress has power to override a decision of the Supreme Court by making new laws or amending the Constitution.

This is not done often but it happens on occasion. In 1793, in a case known as *Chisholm* v. *Georgia,* the Court ruled that the citizens of a state have the right to sue another state in federal court. People were so outraged by this decision, which limited state independence, that the 11th Amendment was added to the Constitution to override this verdict.

What's to keep the justices from being swayed in their opinions by those who appoint them and set their salaries? For one thing, justices are appointed for life terms. They cannot be fired when a new President is elected. Congress can impeach a justice, which means forcing them to step down after a trial in the Senate. Only serious misconduct could cause Congress to do this. And judges' salaries cannot be cut. As a result, the justices are free to voice their opinions without fearing for their jobs.

There are three types of cases that come before the Supreme Court. The first, and least common, involves foreign diplomats or state governments. The second type consists of cases that have been appealed after a verdict has been reached in the lower federal courts. The final category is made up of appeals from state supreme courts in cases involving a federal matter. This means a constitutional right may have been denied or granted by the state.

It wasn't until 1803, under Chief Justice John Marshall, that the Court established its authority of "judicial review"—the Court's right to examine the laws and actions of the government and decide if they are in keeping with the Constitution of the United States. As President Adams was preparing to leave office in 1801, he appointed several judges to make sure the judiciary remained Federalist, despite the political views of the incoming Republican president, Thomas Jefferson.

After Jefferson assumed office, he refused to allow the Secretary of State, James Madison, to make Adams's choices official. One of the appointed justices, William Marbury, brought suit against Madison. Chief Justice Marshall and his associate justices declared that it was against the Constitution—"unconstitutional"—for President Jefferson to prevent Marbury from becoming a justice. This famous case, called *Marbury* v. *Madison,* established the Court's authority to

117

interpret the Constitution and declare laws of Congress and acts of the president unconstitutional.

The Constitution did not specify the number of justices to sit on the Court, so Congress decided upon six. This number has changed over the years, increasing to nine in 1869, which it has remained ever since. This number, however, has been challenged many times, most recently in the 1930s. President Franklin Roosevelt wanted to enact a series of economic reforms, entitled the New Deal, to help ease the Great Depression that forced many Americans to live in poverty. The Supreme Court found some aspects of his act to be unconstitutional. Furious that the New Deal would not be allowed, President Roosevelt asked Congress to increase the Court's size by six members. Roosevelt intended to appoint judges who would support his new laws. Congress refused to do this. Shortly after, one of the conservative justices retired. President Roosevelt replaced him with a liberal judge, and the New Deal reforms were enacted anyway.

The Supreme Court is in session from October to June. During this time, approximately 150 cases are heard. Even with this heavy case load, the Court refused to hear many cases. The justices hear lawyers argue cases and hand down decisions for four hours a day, Monday through Thursday. Lawyers from both sides give the justices extensive briefs—written statements—concerning their case. Then they each have half an hour to argue their case and answer the justices' questions.

118

On Wednesday afternoons and all day on Fridays, the justices gather to discuss the cases they have heard. Each justice gives his opinion, starting with the Chief Justice, who also acts as chairperson. After much discussion, the nine members of the Court vote on the issue, with the most recently appointed justice voting first. At the end of the vote, the Chief Justice, if he agrees with the majority, assigns someone to write the Court's opinion. If he differs from the majority opinion, the senior justice on the majority side assigns the written judgement instead. The judges who disagree will usually write a "dissenting judgment."

To help them decide cases, the justices use the doctrine of precedent. When the Supreme Court was newly founded, there were no previous constitutional cases for the justices to base their decisions upon. The justices were forced to judge cases using only their own interpretations of the Constitution. They had tried to be fair. After each case was decided, their reasoning was carefully recorded. Decades later, justices used these previous rulings to make decisions in new cases that were similar to the old ones. This insures that the laws are consistent over long periods of time. Sometimes, a justice may not personally agree with the way a verdict had been reached in the past, but will still rule on a similar case in the same way. This doctrine of law that binds the courts to follow precedent is known by the latin words *stare decisis* (pronounced STAR-ay dee-SY-sis).

Only on extremely rare occasions has the Supreme

Court broken with this practice. In the case of *Brown* v. *Board of Education of Topeka* in 1954, the justices held that public schools could not be segregated on the basis of race. The Court was forced to overturn some of its own earlier decisions, because those precedents discriminated against African-Americans. In order to have racial equality in America, the judges agreed that in this one important case they had to depart from the doctrine of *stare decisis.*

Until the 1930s, the Court's main emphasis was on regulating industry and economics. After this time, the Court became more involved with individual civil rights. The 1966 case of *Miranda* v. *Arizona* established the famous "Miranda Warnings," which are the rights that police officers must read to suspects before arresting them. In *Roe* v. *Wade* in 1973, the Court decided that women have a constitutional right to choose to have an abortion. Today, some people want the Supreme Court to overrule *Roe* v. *Wade.* To do this, however, the Court would have to break with the tradition of *stare decisis.*

As times change, so does the Supreme Court. Controversy will always surround it because of the great power it possesses over the Constitution and the nation. There will always be dissenters and arguments. But for as long as there is a Constitution to be enforced, the Supreme Court must determine what is just and fair.

Other books you might enjoy reading

1. Coolidge, Olivia. Women's Rights: The Suffrage Movement in America. Dutton, 1966.

2. Forte, David F. The Supreme Court. Franklin Watts, 1979.

3. Gersh, Harry. Women Who Made America Great. Lippincott, 1962.

4. Ingraham, Claire R. An Album of Women in American History. Franklin Watts, 1972.

5. Levenson, Dorothy. Women of The West. Franklin Watts, 1973.

6. Powell, Lawrence Clark. Arizona. W.W. Norton & Company, Inc., 1976.

About the Author

Beverly Berwald teaches at a Child Guidance Clinic when she's not writing or concocting recipes. She lives in Sherman Oaks, California, along with her faithful companion, her computer.